Brāhmanic Vignettes

Other books by the author

1. Jambudwipa, A Blueprint For A South Asian Community. New Delhi: Radiant Publishers, 1986.
2. Bharat Darshana. Hongkong: High Commission of India, 1964.
3. Manasasarowar. Mysore: Hill Temple Publications, 1986.

Brāhmanic Vignettes

Diplomat's Nostalgia

by
"Ācharya of Vidya Kula"

With a Foreword by Dr. Karan Singh,
Member Rājya Sabha and President
Indian Council for Cultural Relations

V. Siddharthacharry

PARTRIDGE
A Penguin Random House Company

To order additional copies of this book, contact
Partridge India
000 800 10062 62
www.partridgepublishing.com/india
orders.india@partridgepublishing.com

To
Magdalen College, Oxford University, England
and
Ācharyā Vidyā Kulā, Mysore, India

ACKNOWLEDGEMENTS

All I owe is to All

The Omniscient sent me Sri Lakshminarasimha Jayaram Haravu. He tried for years to prevail upon me to share with others my experiences. They had, he said, given him much joy, and he became the propeller of my craft. He has been devoting all his time and effort to bring forth the Vignettes; and is fully responsible for the delivery of the infant who was gestated for 9 decades. My gratitude to him, as midwife, is profound.

While I have dedicated to the book to two Fanes of Learning. They include the personalities in them who provided me the ability and capacity needed to share the harvest for which they are responsible. Three persons to whom I shall remain indebted are Sri. N.M. Chandrashekar, Sri. D. Dayananda and Sri. Ram Prasad. They have put up with my singularities in good humour. My gratitude also to Smt. Divya Changappa for painstaking proof reading done by her.

I am deeply grateful to the Hon'ble Dr. Karan Singhji for providing the Vignettes with a Foreword. A scholar in Sanskrit, he was, in every sense, an Ambassador of India and also actually, our Head of Mission in Washington, D.C. After Indian independence and Kashmir's accession to India, he was Sadar-i-Riyasat of Kashmir. He has written several books, one of them, autobiographic. He is a Sanskritophone. Presently, he is a member of the Rajya Sabha.

Andal Thamasavathi, née Keshava Iyengar, is my wife. Her memory has been invaluable to me in authoring the Vignettes. Her patience, throughout the production of the Vignettes, permitted barely 60 minutes out of 1440 every day and night of my company. It has, I feel, to be gratefully preserved and acknowledged.

Dr. Karan Singh

MEMBER OF PARLIAMENT
RAJYA SABHA
(UPPER HOUSE OF PARLIAMENT)

PRESIDENT
INDIAN COUNCIL FOR
CULTURAL RELATIONS
(ICCR)

Foreword
by
Dr. Karan Singh

It is a pleasure to re-engage with Shri Siddharthacharry whom I have known in several of our incarnations. When I was at Doon School from 1942-1946 I have the good fortune of having him as our English teacher. Among all the teachers that I encountered during those four years, Shri Siddharthacharry was, by far, the most outstanding. His classes were not dry discourses but presentations full of passion and energy. He was particularly fond of poetry and would read long poems which the class, uncharacteristically, heard in complete silence. The fact that now seventy years later I can still recite poetry in several languages is, I think, due in a large measure to Shri Siddharthacharry's influence.

Our second encounter was when I was Sadar-e-Riyasat and Shri Siddharthacharry was in the Foreign Service. I must admit that I was rather surprised to find him in a bureaucratic position as I had thought that he was really cut out to be a Professor or a Vice-Chancellor. However, he seems to have enjoyed his stint in the Foreign Service and indeed this book is largely about his diplomatic nostalgia.

After that we kept vaguely in touch until one year when he invited me to visit the estimable Institute that he has set up in Mysore called 'Acharya Vidya Kula' which is envisaged on the lines of the ancient Ashramas, with special emphasis on Sanskrit and spiritual values. I was deeply impressed with this Institute and it is good to know that at 93 Shri Siddharthacharry is still actively managing it.

In this personal background I am happy to present to readers his unusual biographical book which, in his own rather quirky manner, he has entitled 'Brahmanic Vignettes: A Diplomat's Nostalgia'. It records his fascinating journey over nine decades, including his childhood, his education and his career, including the period at Doon School. The book includes perceptive essays on India's foreign policy, a detailed account of the liberation of Goa and, perhaps most interesting of all, his personal reminiscence of people like Dr. Radhakrishnan, Ho Chi Minh, Julius Nyrere and Sarojini Naidu. He ends with his canine encounters, leading finally to his core interest in Vedantic values in education and, as a good Vaishnava, with the Ramayana.

All in all this is the testament of a highly intelligent, intellectually passionate and spiritually oriented human being whom I have had the privilege of knowing over the last seventy years.

Karan Singh

PROLOGUE

Om tat sat. Tat twam asi
That is Truth. That thou art

At the still unripe age of 93, I am not attempting an autobiography: I am still but an infinitesimal in the Infinite. Like all things, I change all the time. Willy-nilly, I shall continue to do so till my life's' end. Fortunately, my dreams, past and present, have been gradually eroding the insulation of **Ahamkārā,** (Egoism). I am Matter but do not matter. Quantum leaps out of one's genes are not normally found in Nature. Only steady evolution during a series of chrysalises produces perfection.

The subject of the anecdotes which follow have had an impact on me: I am the less egoistic in consequence. Autobiographies are seldom accurate, seldom efficacious, rarely even amusing. They will have, hopefully, sketched the gradual approach to my sole objective in life: to be thoroughly **Brāhmanic.** But, what is being "Brāhmanic?" (vide Appendix-I).

It means that I should: discard **Desire**; cease to **Want**; gradually need **Nothing** by merger into **Everything**, the **ALL**, the Infinite, the *Parabrahman.* That is *Sat Chit Ānandam* (complete Bliss), the only goal devoutly to be reached. It is as well to assume that every individual: human, vegetable, mineral is pure energy, essentially indestructible. Man's privilege is to dis-cover within oneself the **Antarayāmin** *Jeevātma,* a Boson, infinitesimal in the Infinite which alone is the indivisible *Parabrahman.* That begets *Paramānandam*, Bliss.

Obviously, the foregoing is an assumption. Certainly, we are not 'believers:' Belief is based upon Ignorance. Belief has been the base of transient religions. Instead, based upon rationality, *Gnyánā* (Gnosis), it is possible and incumbent for the infinitesimal thinking being, Man, to evolve into the Infinite.

I can think of no better description of the characteristics of the Enlightened One, than verses 55-72 of the 2nd adhayā (canto) of the

Bhagawad Geeta given as answers to Arjuna's questions by Lord Krishna. (Appendix-VI).

My immediate objective is to influence school–leavers, particularly those of Āchāryā Vidyā Kulā[1], founded in the turmoil of the last century. Because of that turmoil, through Āchāryā Vidyā Kulā's alumni and similar products of similar schools, it is possible that the GOLDEN AGE, better defined as **Satya Yuga,** Epoch of Truth, may again be ushered. For, Time is increasingly speeding towards the end of the Leaden Age back to the Golden Age.

We are already in the **antamapāda,** the final quarter of **Kali yuga**, the rusting Iron Age. Hence the purpose of Indian schools should be to preserve and educate the remnants of Indian culture, '**Samskriti**', to harbingers of **Satya Yuga**.

The Vignettes in this book cover about 90 years from 1923, when I was 3 years old. They may not be in chronological but, hopefully, in logical order. Inevitably, there would be repetition to make each Vignette complete in itself. However, to avoid making any Vignette more than 15 minutes of reading, they are made distinctively into two or even three parts if they relate to the same subject or episode. In Sanskrit, I would call the Vignettes, **Darshanāḥ:** (Spiritual observations)

---

[1] *Ācharya Vidyā Kulā (AVK)* (www.Āchāryavidyakula.org) *is a school founded by the author in Mysore, India. The school is under the umbrella of the Indian Council for Secondary Education (ICSE). An experiment in value education started by the author called* **Dharmamananam** *has had interesting results (see Vignettes 60, 61).*

VISHISHTA ADVAITA

Modified Monoism

Tossed upon the waves of feckless Chance
Or upon Dilemmas' horns
Life leads us all a merry dance
Every crown in-set with thorns

Tomorrow's ever is the hopeful hour
After Today's sweated labour
But naught is ever in our power
Nor thank Heaven, in our neighbour's!

Seated snugly on the hub of Time
We glorify the dust we raise
Reason we summon, sometime rhyme,
To gull all others with self-praise!

Better surely it is to weave a dream
Than seek quenching water holes
In mirages they are not what they seem
While we play our bonded roles.

We may modify the illusion
Of our little Kaleidoscope
Of existence and attempt fusion
Knowing the serpent to be but a rope

Let us let ourselves gracefully yield
To Chronos' gleaning sickle
We, grains scattered in his field
Out of precious little making muckle

V. Siddharthacharry

We are seated in MAYA's galley ship
Bound for KARMA's distant port;
We must follow Dharmic charts for our trip
And act our parts in Cosmic Story
For we remain in the Eternal script.

CONTENTS

BACKGROUND AND FAMILY

Vignette 1. Indic Society

The foundation of the Indic Society, as Toynbee defined it, was the **Joint Family**. It had many advantages and few disadvantages. There has always been the possibility of escape from the Joint Family. Indeed it was prescribed that one ought to retire, towards the end of one's span of life, to a hermitage or become an itinerant *Sanyāsi*. Joint families enabled specialization in various vocations necessary for Society at no expense to Society at large. For instance, *Gharanās* of Indian Music and temples fostering dances of various Schools, such as *Bharathanātyam*, have, for millennia, been providing the highest exponents of these Arts. **Maystris** (artisans) who have built Temples, Palaces, Tombs (including the Taj Mahal), evolved the architecture and construction of all Indian buildings, including making the material for buildings, economically because of the Joint Families. *Ayurvedā* (Indian Herbal Medicine) also depended upon the Joint Family. It still does in Kerala, S.W. India.

Agriculture, basic industry at all times for all Societies, has been predominant in India in its villages. This was done successfully until this century also because of the virtual Joint Family. So-called Globalization, euphuism for Global plutocracy, is killing it.

The consequence of the vocational family was CASTE[2]. Usually, a group of five villages, until recently, did not compete. They complemented and supplemented each other. Artisanship (Industry) supplied all communities of *Panchagrāmah* (five villages) their basic needs. *Panchagrāmah* begot every successful form of local Government most Democratically. Contrarily, Political Parties compel citizens to vote for nominees chosen by the former and vested interests, and not for those whom citizens themselves choose. Vested interests are viciously either bribe givers or bribe takers. Thus, Governments are oligarchic,

---

[2] *The term* **Caste** *is of Portuguese origin. It is cognate with the Latin* **casta** *signifying "chastity" or "purity." The caste system became religious after having being Vocational. Vocation became religious.*

and essentially, plutocratic; one could add theocratic when religious potentates combine with monarchy or plutocracy to secure Absolute Power which corrupts them absolutely. Truly Indic Governance, through Joint Family and Artisanal Caste, precluded Pseudo-Democracy.

Living close to Nature, Indic Society provided, through *Ayurvedā*, simple cures for simple diseases, prescribed by family Doctors. A sub-caste became expert in furnishing bodily relief. Families developed both theory and practice of Music and Dance. This enabled attainment of unsurpassable peaks. Teaching expertise too was handed down the generations. Revered Wisdom and learning earned food, clothing and shelter. It was Oekonomia non-pareil; it was both efficient and economic.

One necessity, Defence from external incursions, and avoidance of internal chaos, was provided by what can be termed the State. The Caste system played an important role. Until recently, the second Caste, were the *Kshatriyās*, to which rulers and soldiers belonged. They sacrificed, without second thought, everything. Limited governance was needed for different types of training and use of simple weapons. When warfare became vicious, through the wherewithal for mass and unscrupulous destruction (e.g., Hiroshima and Nagasaki), manufacture and sale of weapons created billionaires. This explains why Pentagons exist in all "Great Powers." *Panchāyat* and *Panchagrāmah* became disempowered.

VIGNETTE 2. DISJOINTED FAMILY

The basis of the Indic Way of Life was the Joint Family. It was intact till my father's birth in 1893. All male offspring of all generations were brought up in the Home. It happened that the numbers including all, spouses, sons and daughters till they were married, lived as a single family, headed by the senior most man for External, and senior most woman for Home Affairs. They were often husband and wife. Otherwise, if the senior husband died, it was the wife of the most senior male who wielded the distaff. However, the senior most widow continued to be given priority. Women were superior within the Home, and managed all matters of the domestic economy. They initiated marriages also. Hence there was no possibility of subjugation of women within the home. Outside the home, it was the other way round; men ruled; they had merely reigned at home. At times, the "King" did try to rebel. There were certain cases of intimidation by the Mother Superior over the ewes of the flock.

Indian economy was fundamentally agricultural. In the Indic Society, Vocation determined Class. Intellect and spirituality had priority; Defence followed; third came the Economy; finally, it was Physical Labour. This was the upside for each of these categories. The downside of the first class, Brāhmanā, was paucity of possessions and total absence of affluence. The second, Kshatriya, was complete dependence on the three others for their expensive living as compensation for readiness to risk life in Defence of the State from without, and for Tranquillity within. The third category, Vyshya, minded both manufacture of necessary artefacts and their distribution. Excelling in that duty they were subject to all the vagaries of the Economy, and fluctuated from immense wealth to utter poverty and *vice versa*. The fourth category were Shudra. It's Upside was that they supplied their own absolute necessities of food, clothing and shelter. The Downside was the strain of doing so. It's strength lay in its being the most populous, and producer and provider of the staple food for all.

This was the Caste system: Brāhmaṇa, Kshatriya, Vaishya and Shudra. Yet another category was the Panchama, or the fifth. They voluntarily did not accept the duties which bound the preceding four. The word, Panchama, apart from meaning 'fifth', in the Indic Society paralleled **Pagans** in the Greco-Roman Society. Pagan means those outside the fence *(Pagus)*. In the rest of the European Society, they were called Heathens, people living on the heaths, and did not conform to the mores of villages, towns and cities. Gonds of Andhra and Madhya Pradesh, as observed by Verrier Elvin[3],[4],[5], had an age-old way of living with a complex life style. The Brāhmanic ethos commands that there should be no attempt at homogeneity by bringing into the Indic Society, others who have a different outlook. Thus the attempt to interfere with so-called primitive society is anathema and self-defeating. Why should we interfere with others, any more than we would permit others to interfere with our way of life?

It is interesting that the English word Caste is derived from the Portuguese Casta which in turn derived from the Latin word meaning Chastity. Every one of the Indic Society had chastely and purely to adopt that vocation of the category into which he or she was born. Thus, a Brāhmanā wouldn't aim at being a king or a shudra being a teacher except in rarest of circumstances and not as the objective of life. This is so because, individual evolution, the only worthy goal is to merge into the Infinite out of infinitesimality, not to attempt to create 'Heaven' on Earth. Presently, having plunged into the nadir of the KALI YUGA, the Rusting Iron Age, the Joint Family, both in the domestic and the social sense, has collapsed. Evidence therefore is being provided by World History. Till about 1870, India & China, accounted for almost 3-quarters of the World's Trade. Thereafter, their Oekonomoeia was shattered.

---

[3]   *Leaves from the jungle: life in a Gond village.* Oxford University Press, 1992.

[4]   *Songs of the Forest; The Folk Poetry of the Gonds.* with Shamrao Hivale. London: G. Allen & Unwin, ltd, 1935.

[5]   *It is an interesting speculation that Dravidians were not the original races in the Deccan. If they are non-Aryan, they are also not of the same races as say the Gonds or Todas. The Greek legend of the disappearance of Atlantis and Gondwanaland, like all legends, must have a cause. A nuclear war between two highly developed continents, such as could well happen again, between Eastern Asia and North America could account for the vanishing of two societies.*

Chaos is approaching. No wonder the golden Sovereign no longer reigns any more than did its Farthing. The gold standard is now not merely a fraction; it is simply not there!

Inherited remnants of the Joint Family account for my being what I am. I was the favoured and only grandson of my paternal grandfather. He educated me traditionally; my teachers in schools instructed me. While I am grateful to the latter, I am percolated by the former. My objective in life remains what I have already stated: Infinity. Now, in my life's horizon, my objective is to see that at least a handful of truly educated youth will form the nucleus of the approaching Golden Age: the East is brightening Tung Fang Hung[6]

> *If a country is to be corruption free and become*
> *a nation of beautiful minds, I strongly feel*
> *there are three key societal members who*
> *make a difference. They are the father, the*
> *mother and the teacher.*
>
> *Abdul Kalam*

---

[6] *The first words of the anthem of revolutionary China!*

Vignette 3. Disjointed family-II

I missed most of the advantages of a Joint Family. My father had decided, when I was 9, to shift from India to Malaya near Singapore in the un-federated Sultanate of Johore of which the capital was Johore Bahru. My mother remained in Mysore. There were only the 3 of us; my paternal grandfather aged 62; my father 40 and I. We had a helper, Govindan,—I avoid the word servant—from Kerala. Our language was Tamil, Govindan's Malayalam. My grandfather had retired when 55 from the British Indian Army Audits and Accounts Department. He had reached the peak of his career. His wife, my grandmother, Janaki, had passed away when I was 7 ½ in Patna (Bihar). I was lucky in having my grandfather all to myself. I called him Pappa. He became the sole source of the wealth of Indian knowledge available to us, teachers of Sanskrit lore and following the Sanskritic Dharma, Way of Life. He had been brought up, till 15, in a small village, Panapākam, near Nellore not far from Chennai, then called Chennapatnam and Madras by the English.

Pappa cooked superbly. All male children of a Brāhmanā family, that had no daughters, had to learn how to cook because, when their mothers were *periodically* prohibited from doing so. She instructed her sons, sitting outside the kitchen how to cook each dish. I owe to Pappa my initiation into our Dharma. Among Christians, it would be Confirmation. I was thus initiated as an Āchārya.

Pappa (in Tamil): "*Never Desire; don't **want** anything specially; want always only not to **want**: you shall get everything you need to live if you lead a **Dharmic** life, worthily. Pray; but for naught, but to be of the Infinite. We are teachers. We must be taught and continue to the end of our lives to teach ourselves and, incidentally, others. Your goal in the game of life is to improve yourself. Tomorrow you must be better than you were yesterday. And this must go on till the last breath of life.*"

Not only did I welcome this behest, I have found Happiness in consequence. This initiation would normally have been done when I went through the ceremony which would entitle me to wear my

Yagnyopavitham, the sacred thread of 3 handloom strings for bachelors and 6 for the married.

As we were stepping out of the house one day, when we got to the threshold, Pappa abruptly held my shoulder and said; *"Be careful, there is a column of ants going to their tasks somewhere. Be careful not to hurt a single one."* This command was, all my life, my guide. *"Always tell the truth, lest you confuse the cells in your brain; they will not be able to distinguish false from true. Worst of all, you yourself will not know what is good or what is bad."* This advice too has stood me in good stead; even as a diplomat, I did not "lie abroad," as the quixotic Englishman said some centuries ago. *"**Satyameva jayate**,"* motto of Indian symbol of three lions, is 'Truth always wins.' Another advice: *"As an Āchārya, you will never be in need of anything. Your wife will see to it. There is no work better than any other, provided it is perfect; it is the same whether you are a Prime Minister or a Scavenger. The latter can actually be better than a Prime Minister; it is easier for him to be perfect."* In life, I have found that, in my own home I am an excellent Scavenger. I doubt if I "excelled" when I was 'his Excellency', the Ambassador of India' in some half-a-dozen countries. Such was my **Up**-bringing by my dearest Pappa. He is, certainly, not dead in me.

Without Analysis no proper Synthesis is possible. Fortunately, I had a fine example when I was 8. We lived in Patna. Father was mad about cars and bought a Citroën. He drove it into a tree. That damaged the Engine. As the Citroën was the first of its kind in Patna, no regular automobile workshop would undertake its repair. He decided that it should be dismantled, and students from the Automobile Engineering Faculty of the University should do so in our garden. All the parts were taken apart and reassembled. I eagerly made myself available to fetch and carry. I saw all the parts being re-assembled. I found out how the car worked: the Analysis enabled Synthesis. Why not apply that to Metaphysics?

P.S.: I too, as my father was, became an automobile maniac. I did not drive into a tree. I did a more foolish thing. I simply would not permit anyone to overtake me. My real career was chauffeuring. At 85, my wife dismissed me because she found, I was a weakling.

Dharma destroys him who destroys Dharma.
Dharma protects him who protects it.
Therefore abandon not your Eternal Dharma.

Vignette 4. Āchāryas

I am descendant of a Joint Family whose Vocation was Teaching. *Āchārya*, our name, signifies Teacher of metaphysics, even as 'Smith' denotes, in English, 'metal worker.' 'Āchārya is also used for the three great Gurus: ***Shankarāchārya, Rāmānujāchārya and Madhwāchārya***. My family does not pretend to such scholarship.

My ancestors lived 2000 years ago in North India then under ***Chakravarthi*** (Emperor) Harshavardhana (5th/6th AC). He sent them south in small family groups of different ***Gothrās*** [7] to spread knowledge and use of Sanskrit beyond the Vindhya Range. They were told to acquire mastery of the regional language; proceed to write outstandingly in them; complementing the ***Prākrits*** (local languages) with Sanskrit terms. Most Prakrit's, barring Tamil, had inadequate vocabularies. Eventually, even Tamil was enriched through Sanskrit. Gradually, Ideas contributed by the ***Vedas***, ***Vedānga*** and ***Mahā Kāvyas*** (epics)—Rāmåyana, Mahābhåratha and Bhāgavatha—were introduced. Thus did India acquire its relatively homogeneous culture. It surpassed what Latin and Greek achieved in

---

[7]   ***Gothras****: literally the word implies Cow-sheds! Teachers are expected not to have anything more treasured than milch-cows and calves. Actually the Gothra is derived from a supposed ancestor. In my case it is **Harida Maharishi**. The male line carries on the Gothra. Marriage of a couple of the same **Gothra** is not permitted. Those who are even more finicky don't even appreciate marriage between cousins of the same **Gothra** as their mothers' were. There is no word for cousin. We are all elder or younger brothers: in Tamil **Annā** or **Tambi** for elder brother and younger brother; **Akka** and **Tangé** for cousin sisters. Till my grandfather married, boys were married to girls from the same village or a neighbouring one. Marriage was before teenage but the couple lived with their own parents till they were old enough to do live as a married couple. There was no divorce.Even before formal marriage, an equally important ceremony, **Nischitārtham** (engagement) was, in practice, as final as marriage. Shame on which ever family resiled! That Joint Family was sent to Coventry.*

Europe. The task, however, is without end. It continues by teaching Sanskrit in various Institutions of learning, minor and major. My ancestors moved from region to region of **Dakshina Pātha** (Deccan). Starting from their first hermitage in Amaravathi, in what is now Maharashtra, my ancestors moved to Thelangana in Āndhra, to Madurai in Tamilnadu, and finally moved to Mysore where I live.

My forbears learnt local languages perfectly. (Alas, my Kannada totters even as my legs do. I left Mysore when I was three and returned when I retired). My maternal grandparents had settled in Mysore State for long and hardly spoke in Tamil. I am proud to have been born in Mysore and was therefore, a subject of one of the finest rulers in World History, Maharaja Krishna Raja Wadiyar).

My paternal grandfather onwards, we fostered English in lieu of Sanskrit, as I did 70 years ago. I am now trying to make amends. Sanskrit has been made obligatory in Āchārya Vidya Kula from Kindergarten up to Std. X and by supporting the ICSE. The unique **Devanāgari** (Sanskrit script) enables exact pronunciation of English and, even better, French. Of necessity, Sanskrit has been used in our experiment, Dharmamananam (vide, Vignette 60, 61) for children, 12-13 years old, in introducing Vedantic metaphysics. Results are promising.

In Vedanta, the Idea that in-forms us is the elucidation of what is vaguely term called 'GOD' but not defined. It is assumed that God is simply the COSMOS. The vulgar adjectives (in the Roman sense) applied to 'GOD', and common all the world over are Infinity of Space, Time and Idea. They are all uncreatable and, together, play a cardinal role in existence. The first two are easily understood. Endlessness in Numbering too is also understood, comprehended and, eventually, realized. 'Idea' is harder to conceive. Split up as **Id** + **Ea**, in Latin (derived from Greek), it is equivalent to the Sanskrit **Tat Sat**, the (whole) Truth. '**Om Tat Sat**', put briefly and as precisely as possible, implies that there can be only One: viz., 'ALL'. Naturally, it is incomprehensible by the infinitesimal but realizable when the individual evolves into the Infinite.

The great Āchāryas taught that it is misleading to think of God anthropomorphically. Actually there was 'Creation', no 'Creator.' Misconception was in considering 'GOD' as a kind of Superman. It led to the absurd Idea that Jupiter or Jove (derived from Jehovah) could be prayed to as if "He" were an earthly monarch. Anthropomorphisation of 'GOD' led to deification of all the Powers ascribed to 'Him'. Logically this led to every one of 'His Powers' also being anthropomorphised.

11

God, being the Idea of Total Power, has no sex, male, female or neuter. Religion invented 'Trinities'; Jupiter-Neptune-Pluto; **Brahma-Vishnu-Maheshwara**; 'God'-Son-Holy Ghost. Then followed Prophets, Saviours and **Avatarās** of Divinity. Vedanta is based on '**Dharma**', proper conduct, as against theism. This implies that all personal actions lead to consequences, desirable or not, depending upon doer and the deed. What is important and relevant to man is that his own **Karma**, (deeds) are consequential. One enjoys or suffers depending upon his deeds in the past, present and future lives. Most religions depend upon the continued existence of Soul, but they do not accept previous birth. Surely, if the Soul can have existence in the **future**, it also can exist in the **past**? Karmic Law is supreme. No amount of prayer to an anthropomorphic Deity or Deities can alter Karmic consequences.

> '*The Moving Finger writes; and having writ;*
> *Moves on: nor all thy piety nor Wit*
> *Shall lure it back to cancel half a line,*
> *Nor all thy Tears wash out a Word of it.*'
> (Rubāiyāt of Omar Khayyām)

The 'Moving Finger' is Karma. **Vedānta** itself means that which flows from Wisdom, the **Vedas**. Obviously, if the Idea of 'GOD' included omnipresence; there is no room for evil (Satan); therefore there is no space for 'HELL.' "God" is the Absolute and **ALL**. Its negation is insubstantial.

I was brought up to consider that the surreptitiously materialistic objective of 'Religion' is sheer theocracy: to control the minds of people catechismatically in the easiest and cheapest way. What has eventually transpired is that the worst and most noxious acts of Man were motivated by the religion, whether through Wars or Inquisitions or Apartheid. Conversion to religions is, therefore, anathema. Individual Freedom of Thought and Speech has been compromised by Religions. One concludes that negation of the ALL (i.e. God) actually leads egoistically absolutely to monopolize power over Mankind and, so, be absolutely corrupted.

Such ideas were immense help in the profession that circumstances led me to, Diplomacy. I felt that as we were all infinitesimals in Infinity, divisions into Countries or Nations were passing shows, not substantial things.

For in out, above, about below,
T'is nothing but a Magic Shadow-show
Play'd in a Box whose Candle is the Sun,
Round which we Phantom Figures come and go.'

Rubaiyāt

While Sufic Khayyam negates, ShankarĀchārya had given the remedy positively:

Mayam idam akhilam buddhva,
Bramha padam pravisha viditva

Bhaja Govindam

(Having wisely learnt that all is a mirage, follow the path that leads you to the Source of ALL)

I was at home everywhere. I loved all my very different assignments: Congo (Zaire) and China, England and Singapore, as much as did my own India. By habit, I have been more at home in Mysore than anywhere else, physically and socially. Mentally and Spiritually I am necessarily Global. I would have been happy working anywhere and, most of all, for **ALL**.

You have to grow from the inside out.
None can teach you, none can make you spiritual.
There is no other teacher but your own soul.

Swami Vivekananda

Vignette 5. Contemporary Up-bringing

In this epoch, **Kali Yuga**, (the Iron Age), to be Brāhmanic, one has to live a double life: Inner and Outer. The Inner and real Aim is to rejoin the **Parabrahman**. The Outer is to specialize in a career suited to him provided it is clearly understood that it is, as it were, only an Act in the Drama of Life. Every actor should act well; if a Chauffeur, he should drive well; if a Teacher, teach well. To be a Brāhmanā, it is easiest to reconcile the Outer and the Inner by teaching well. Originally, the highest form of teaching was expected to be that of a metaphysicist. Shakespeare's Seven Ages of Man, spoken by Jacques in As You Like It, is only a joke. The real Aim of the Inner is perfection of character. The Outer must not compromise the Inner at any cost. Metaphorically put, it may be better understood: in a cavern after a lapse of time, both stalagmites and stalactites become a single column. So too, in life, perfect Brāhmanism reconciles the terrestrial and the celestial; they merge. When one has attained the Infinite, one's condition is blissful; heavenly. This process is Yogic. Curiously, it is only Polynesian Māna[8] that is nearest to the purpose of Yoga. Normally, only the first step, *Hattha Yoga*, is attempted. This merely prepares the human body, not the mind. There is a sequence of the remaining steps, manifest in the Bhagawad Geeta. Its final (18th), **adhyāya** (canto) is Moksha (realization of the goal).

There were other observations which not merely coloured, but permeated my character. It is the beneficence of Infinity, its power and not mine, that made me gravitate towards the immaculate. That is why the periodical, **Antaryamin** (Inner Self or Soul), is brought out by Āchārya Vidya Kula. Its object was the Education, bringing forth of the Immanent within every child. Even is the bringing out of latent is not Education, it is Instruction. Education is the awakening of dormant

---

[8]   **Māna:** *Firstly, Polynesians were not primitive; they were primaeval. Primeavality was simpler and less contentious than the splitting of "cummin seeds" by 'civilized' scholars seeking to outwit each other.*

Divinity. Apropos, the Vanity of Human Affairs, I can do no better than quote Shelley's, **Ozymandias**

> *I met a traveller from an antique land*
> *Who said: Two vast and trunkless legs of stone*
> *Stand in the desert. Near them on the sand*
> *Half sunk, a shatter'd visage lies, whose frown*
> *And wrinkled lip and sneer of cold command*
> *Tell that its sculptor well those passions read*
> *Which yet survive, stamp'd on these lifeless things,*
> *The hand that mock'd them and the heart that fed;*
> *And on the pedestal these words appear:*
> *'My name is Ozymandias, king of kings:*
> *Look on my works, ye Mighty, and despair!'*
> *Nothing beside remains. Round the decay*
> *Of that colossal wreck, boundless and bare,*
> *The lone and level sands stretch for away.*
>
> -P.B. Shelley

OZYMANDIAS deals beautifully with Transience. It is Negative; the Positive Shelley spells out beautifully in the last lines of his **ADONAIS**:

> *The One remains, the many change and pass;*
> *Heaven's light for ever shines, Earth's shadows fly;*
> *Life, like a dome of many-coloured glass,*
> *Stains the white radiance of Eternity . . .*

Shelley, like Emerson and Thoreau, Boston Brāhmanās, of Massachusetts, U.S.A., were struck by the Vedic Truths relayed by the Asiatic Society of Kolkatta in the early 19th century. Emerson's reference to **Brahma**—"When you him fly, He is the wings!" is a brilliant resumé of **Vedantic** Cosmic Divinity.

> *Great men are they who see that spiritual is stronger*
> *than any material force—that thoughts rule the world.*
> *Ralph Waldo Emerson*

VOYAGES

Vignette 6. Second Voyage-I

Singapore to Tilbury, London, mid-1935

Just before my 15th birthday my father, a WOG[9], decided to send me to England disregarding my grandpa's reaction to being parted from his then only grandchild. Our home had ceased to be in Johore Bahru, the southernmost part of Asia. It moved across the strait, Selat Tebrau. It was within the Singapore Naval Base. Our house was on a promontory overlooking the causeway linking Johore to Singapore. From the cliff, sunrise was to the right and sunset to left. Almost daily, these wonders regaled me, "the growing boy." I still recall them in nostalgic moments. They Informed and educated me as Wordsworth did in his sonnet, **"The World is too much with us . . . ."**

I thought that I had completed schooling 2 years earlier, with a creditable Senior Cambridge Certificate in December 1933 and, in December '34, a Supplementary Certificate in Latin and Greco-Roman History. We had been informed that it was obligatory for admission into English Universities for Arts' students. 1934 was crucial. I had an hour's private tutorial every Thursday afternoon in Singapore by Mr. Tiddemann, teaching in Raffles Institution. Besides, I read two English classics weekly during the 18 months before I left for school in Ashburton, South Devon, S.W. England. Not far from Ashburton was, to me, the attractive Dartmoor. It is famous for its wild ponies, and notorious for England's most feared prison whence the escapes of die-hard criminals were, from time to time, hot news for the Media. The river Dart was a 20-minute walk away from the '**Wilderness**', the home

---

[9]   *WOG: Western Oriented Gentleman, Rudyard Kipling's naughty but apt description of Indians who not only worked for the English ruler but acted like Sahibs. An important result of this was that assigned peons had to greet them in the morning not with Namaste and folded hands but "Salaam Saab" clicking heels and a smart salute.*

of my host and Headmaster of Wilderness School. When I left it was less appealingly called Ashburton College. The Dart was a lovely stream with a beautiful granite bridge. Many happy summer and autumn mornings and evenings were spent sitting on one of the several rocks that spangled the crystal and shallow brook gurgling past, lovely little fish always nibbling at toes trailing in the water.

I left Malaya and Singapore at the end of June 1935 to reach Tilbury, London's port, on 25ᵗʰ July. This was my second voyage. The first had been in January 1930 along with my grandpa on the SS: Egra from Kolkatta to Rangoon, (now Yangon), in Burma, (now Myanmar) and continued on the SS: Tilawa to Singapore. The second voyage was on a Japanese liner, Fushimi-Maru of the Nippon Yusen Kaisha (NYK). I was the only Indian and youth on board. I had the privilege of being the ward and guest of the Captain at lunch and dinner. Fellow passengers were mostly English, homeward bound, relatively cheaply with their wives and children. Being only in the first half of my teens, I was popular with the ladies. They were happy to entrust their children to me because they adored me. The eldest of the little ones was about 8; the youngest 3, of whom I welcomed special charge. It was excellent apprenticeship for distant parenthood and immediate future as parlour-boarder[10].

Delightfully for me, Fushimi-Maru was a cargo-passenger. She ploughed the waves as leisurely as I could wish. Voyaging was familiar, because of my Greek History and Literature, with Ulysses/Odysseus. All my voyages have been as joyful as his were not. Fushimi-Maru was boarded at dusk. My father accompanied me for early dinner at 6 pm. He compelled me, for the first time in my life, to eat non-vegetarian offal. Tearfully I ate. Hurrah! Father had to go because the siren for departure shouted to him to hurry up and leave the ship. I was thankful and threw

---

[10] *Parlour–Boarder: I don't find the word in any Dictionary. Yet it is common usage in England. It is considered a more suave word than* **Paying Guest** *or even just* **P.G.** *in Indian English. Being admitted to both to the family dining table and family drawing room called the* **Parlour** *meaning a place where you could talk in homely manner was a great privilege naturally, paid for sumptuously. In the Parlour, the fire-place would warm you from mid-autumn right up to the end of spring whereas in dormitories one could be reasonably comfortable one could take off the overcoat from the beginning of the winter in January till its end in March.*

up the whole dinner; with that my sin was expunged. (I have remained Brāhmanically vegetarian except, perhaps, whenever I didn't know what I was eating!).

Being a cargo-passenger, our ship stopped frequently *en route* to discharge cargo. Our first halt was Port Swettenhan (now **Kelang**) the following morning. It was then British territory, part of Straits Settlements along with Singapore, Malacca, Dindings and Penang. Kelang is now the outlet for Kuala Lumpur, present capital of Malaysia. It was not prepossessing. Having been schooled in Malaya, I knew a bit of its History. Before the British, it had been Dutch; a couple of centuries earlier, Portuguese. Earlier still, the Kalingā Empire had used all the west Malayan ports except Singapore which did not then exist. Some centuries earlier, Kālingan merchant-adventurers, based in today's Odissa, near Bengal sailed from Puri. They made themselves at home in all Ports. Malaya was so named, from Sanskrit, because of being hilly, though not mountainous like Himalaya. The Kālingan's were a darker shade of brown than the Malays. As with Javanese their language, Malay was also infiltrated by Sanskrit, just as my ancestors had accomplished the marriage of Sanskrit with Marāthi, Kannada, Malayālam, Telugu, and to a considerable extent, Tamil, my mother tongue. Kelang recalls Kālinga. Most other Indian visitors and emigrants to Malaya were from Northern India. They were of lighter shade of brown than the Malayans. The Kālingan's had no doubt been snooty in Malayā and were called "**Klings**" which became a word of abuse. After Malayā's Independence, Tamil Indians were a considerable number and the back-bone of the **Rubber Plantations.** They too were called Klings. As the term was abusive, it was legally outlawed and they were simply called Tamils. Incidentally, the less brown Indians, having left India via Calcutta (now Kolkatta), are all called Bangāli even if obviously Sikhs, turbaned and bearded.

Kālingan merchant-adventurers became part of the **Indian** East India Company, model for the future **European** East Indian Companies. The Kālingan's were not alone as they belonged to the Deccan Consortium, the prototype for the Portuguese, Dutch, English, French and Danish. The Deccan Consortium made Malacca their first port of call. They went as far as New Zealand of which there is evidence in the Auckland Museum. Kelang had been fortified by them. Difference between Indians and Europeans was that the latter had **Guns!**

Fushimi-Maru's next halt was Penang (now Pinang meaning Betel-Nut which was the chief export to India). It is a fascinating Island with a Snake temple approached by a funicular. From Penang skirting Ceylon (now Sri Lanka), we sailed leisurely to Aden leading to the Red Sea. It was instructive to behold the Arab Homeland; desert, oasis, camel ride, searing dusty gusts, clamorous bazaar and, consequently, a happier return to paradise, Fushimi-Maru.

My birthday happened half-way from Aden to Suez at the southern end of the Suez Canal. A cable sent to me from my dearest folk in Malāya was presented to me by the Captain of Fushimi-Maru at a surprise party for me on the starboard deck which had been forbidden to all passengers after Lunch till Tea. It was organized with 'éclat' for all the children and their parents. I doubt if any other than an aesthetically inclined Oriental Shipping Line, the NYK, would have made such a touching gesture. Not all the vilification of the Japanese some 10 years later can wipe out my treasured memory of such delicatesse. However, atrocities were certainly committed.

The Red Sea seemed to have a seabed over a stove; the sea was not just warm but hot. The Air was stifling. We reached Suez. Passengers were told they might, if they wished to leave the ship, rejoin it at Port Saïd at the Northern end of the canal 36-hours later. They could go by cab to see the Great Pyramids and the Sphinx. They had to pay for the cab and more, if they wished to stay the night in a waiting room. Two or three cab-fulls went. I neither could spare the cash nor wished to leave my comfortable cabin. Besides, I looked forward to sailing through the Canal. My decision was wise. The canal trip was exciting in itself. Fushimi-Maru steamed at a snail's pace; at times, alternately, it moored itself larboard in artificial coves to allow on-coming ships to pass. The compliment was repaid by the next on-coming ship. The ship's Captain deserved to be congratulated on his expertise. A ship was barely 10-feet away when passing another or being passed.

Port Saïd itself was reached rather late in the evening after dinner. At dawn we were woken up by a hullabaloo. There was an invasion. We were all told to close the portholes of our cabins and lock the doors. The deck was crammed with vendors and jugglers. Vendors caught hold of passengers by hand and stopped them, to sell almost everything imaginable from matchboxes to what they claimed to be Pharaohs' relics.

These included bangles, teeth and bones taken out of sarcophagi[11], some relics and fish shells supposed to be charms. Most of them, we were told by the ship's officers, would be fake. I bought nothing. The jugglers and acrobats were much more interesting. I did, as asked, throw them a few shillings.

We sailed away from Port Saïd by dusk before dinner. We were in the Mediterranean. I, thanks to my having whiled away almost two years reading Greek and Roman History, the epics Iliad, Odyssey and Aeneid, had my head crammed with stories about wonderful people and wondrous things done by them, in and around the Mediterranean. I had often day-dreamt about them. To be on the Mediterranean was a fulfillment. Mediterranean is so called because the Greeks thought that they were in the Middle of the Earth. All other Europeans agreed. That accounts for their Euro centricity. Historically too, they believed that civilization started in Europe; all other languages were primitive until Europeans spoke. Curiously, Chinese also call their country **Chung Kuo;** meaning, in Chinese, *"**Middle Country**"*!

We sailed to Italy. I had read Lytton's **Last Days of Pompeïi** and the **Life of Savonarola.** I had updated myself through newspapers about the short-lived conquest of Ethiopia by Il Duce[12] (Benito Mussolini). Fushimi-Maru sailed south of Sicily and north of Malta, both historically famous. Our port of call in Italy was Naples. There is the saying; **"See Naples and Die."** I saw, I enjoyed, I still live (at 93).

It was Full-Moon night. Fushimi-Maru was so moored that we beheld Vesuvius, majestically crowned by the Full Moon erupting from its crater, volcanic vapor its petals. Thanks to Il Duce, for a change, Naples, earlier notorious for its disease (VD), ill-kept roads and un-removed rubbish, was seen by us, spick and span, in its pristine glory, the capital of a powerful Duke. Some passengers including me went to visit the excavated cities of Pompeïi and Herculaneum which drowned by Lava. Vesuvius, it seemed, had been enraged by the dissipation of its citizens, both patrician and Plebeian 2000-years ago. They had been preserved dead but intact otherwise by the hard Lava in every kind of

---

[11]   **Sacrophagi:** plural of sarcophagus, a *sculpted container of coffins looted from Pyramids.*

[12]   *Il Duce* इल दुचे : *The Leader. Hitler was referred, to in Germany, as: **Der Führer***

human pose, clothed and unclothed, in various activities both public and very private. No thanks to my immaturity at 15: I was forbidden to views concupiscence even though "enlavaed." I was told all this by a friendly ship's officer.

Vignette 7. Second Voyage-II

Marseilles to Tilbury, London

Our next port was Marseilles. We were allowed ashore only after breakfast and before lunch. I could only admire the port and the cheerful gaiety of the sailors and dockyard workers. Even this begot a happy memory. I was to see similar Dockers some 40-years later in Shanghai and in Hong Kong, (Fragrant Harbour), and my final posting in Singapore. In all of them, I was head of the Indian Diplomatic Missions. In Singapore, most of the dockers are Indians and mostly Tamil. All Shipping Lines agreed that the World's most efficient Dockers were those of Singapore. The Prime Minister, Lee Kuan Yew, was delighted. He elevated their Union Leader, Devan Nair, to the dizzy post of President of Singapore. Alas! Out of that exalted post, he reeled away somewhat sooner than later.

The next halt was Jebel-el-Tariq (Gibraltar), so named after its Ottoman founder. The Head of the Ottoman Empire was called the Caliph. This implied that he was Leader of Muslims. His Capital was **Istanbul**. Earlier it was **Constantinople** named after Constantine who introduced Christianity as the State Religion. Earlier still it was **Byzantium**. The Ottomans were Turks from Turkistan in Central Asia; their original religion was Shaman Buddhism. They were resisted by Arabs who had all embraced Islam. They united against the Turks because they were non-Muslim. Realizing that the Arabs were united only because of their religion, Turks too became Muslims. The Arab states reverted to fighting among themselves. Some of them sought alliance with the Turks. In a few decades, the Ottoman Empire expanded all over Arabic speaking territory right up to the Atlantic Ocean throughout North-Africa.

The Turkish Ottomans became the overlord of the entire Mediterranean. They conceived the prototype of modern naval fleets. Spain, Portugal, France, England and the Dutch in the Netherlands gradually copied the Ottoman model. The head of the Ottoman fleet was called Ameer-al-Bahr (Ruler of the Sea). This was the origin of the

English word Admiral. The rock fort of Gibraltar has been British for a couple of centuries. It is still a hard bone of contention between England and Spain. Many Indian merchants settled in Gibraltar. A notable feature is Gibraltar's apes; it is believed that as long the apes are on the Rock, Gibraltar cannot be conquered. Perhaps the apes had exported themselves from Lanka after having helped the Avatar, Sri Rāma to defeat Rāvana!

Our next stop was Rabat, in Morocco. This northwestern tip of Africa played an outstanding role in the modernization of Europe. The Moors of Morocco were not Arabs. But they learnt Arabic along with their own languages. Arabic became the Official language. The local languages such as Berber continued to be used. The Moors introduced Indian Mathematics which they had learned in Damascus in Syria, into Spain. They copied the work that Pythagoras had started in Sicilian Greece. Their Universities in Andalusia became famous throughout Europe. The Moors at their zenith controlled Spain right up to the Pyrenees. Their architectural expertise and aesthetics as exemplified in Alhambra, Granada, are of the same rank as the Hindu Temple in Madurai and the Taj Mahal in Agra. Another Moorish contribution was their breed of Horses. These are particularly swift on the turn like knights on chessboards. This would have been one of the reasons for being able to worst the cavalry of the West Europeans. The Ottoman Empire used both Arab and Moorish breeds. It was a pleasure to have had a glimpse of the native land of such an enterprising and able people. The bazaars were like those of Northern Indian cities especially Delhi, Lucknow and Allahabad.

Fushimi-Maru reached Tilbury in East London a week later. It was an affecting parting to me. The Captain, Officers and cabin boys still haunt me in nostalgic waking dreams. I had entirely to myself, a 4-berth cabin. This allowed me to change my berths whimsically. I discovered that even at 15+, childish naughtiness was quite a relaxation. Most importantly it was my study. I managed to equip myself with sufficient French to surprise my Head Master, who was skeptical about my being fit for the final examination of the Cambridge School Certificate in December. Every day and half a night, when I was not on the deck playing various games, I studied most diligently, Hugo's French Language Simplified. Its cover page promised the ability to speak French in 6-months. It had a mere 28 lessons, each of about 3-pages. My voyage had lasted for 31 days; so I had 3 days for revision. This was really a stroke of luck. The stroke was duly dealt, respectfully, to my future Head Master, Mr. Naylor. More later, about new surprises for him.

PURSUIT OF EDUCATION

Vignette 8. Parlour-Boarder[13]

Mr. Henry Naylor, Head Master of the Wilderness School, later named Ashburton College, (thank Heaven, after I left), was named after his residence. The main school was across the road. It was 3-storeyed with boarder dormitories on the top floor. Mr. Naylor was my guardian from August 1935 to August '38 when I left for Oxford. It was a large house with a vast garden. It stretched from the Main Street for a whole furlong to the rear, bordering the London-Exeter-Plymouth highway speeding up hill and down dale. On the other side was a modest hill on which cattle grazed, cutting paths on the hillside. The grass looked so luscious that I wished I was a cow. The garden was demi-paradise. Any botanist would have envied us. There was a Gingko Balboa, a Monkey-Puzzle (Chilean pine), a Maple, of course an Oak and a huge and lovely Copper Beech, both radiating and soaring above 20-meters. There were many other trees, as well. The Copper Beech was a canopy for my Studies from mid-spring to end-autumn. I left Wilderness in 1938, and so did the Naylor family, selling it to a Convent. I can't imagine how they could abandon that lovely home. I was glad that I went from demi-paradise to Paradise itself, the vast grounds of Magdalen in Oxford.

---

13   Parlour–Boarder: *I don't find the word in any Dictionary. Yet it is common usage in England. It is considered a more suave word than* **Paying Guest** *or even just* **P.G.** *in Indian English. Being admitted to both to the family dining table and family drawing room called the* **Parlour** *meaning a place where you could talk in homely manner was a great privilege naturally, paid for sumptuously. In the Parlour the fire-place would warm you from mid-autumn right up to the end of spring whereas in dormitories one could be reasonably comfortable one could take off the overcoat from the beginning of the winter in January till its end in March.*

I was cosseted by several families in Ashburton. It was a township of about twenty thousand consisting of middle-class elderly families, mostly ageing spinsters on the wrong side of 50. I was invited along with my foster sister Margaret as her chaperon. They were curious about the brownie who could, the rumour was, actually speak English as well as, if not better than boys of his age in Devon and was being groomed for Oxford. They made me feel at home, and I learnt a lot about such gentry in England. Some even considered me to be the son or grandson of Maharajas. I hastened to disillusion them; my weekly pocket money was only 2 shillings 6 pence, i.e., half a crown, 1/8 of a Pound Sterling, of which 1 shilling paid for my weekly letter to Malaya.

The Naylor family was quarrelsome, especially at the top, husband and wife; at the bottom their 3rd offspring and only daughter, Margaret and 4th, the son, David. The two sons Charles and John were 21 and 20 years old. They studied in London and Oxford respectively. They came back during the holidays. Charles studied Engineering and John, History. What irritated David most was that his sister gave the biggest piece of cake to me and when the fellow Parlour-Boarder, Randolph Boxall, joined us next year, as big a one to him too. Randolph and I became chums. Our friendship burgeoned precociously every year in profusion till we parted for always in 2003. I wrote for his memorial compiled by Marjorie, his dear wife and "Good Companion." I wrote because Marjorie felt that what I wrote about Randolph might be better construed were something about the writer too were known: she could think of none to provide aught credible about me.

I heartily agree with Robert Burns and echo his craving,

O wad some Pow'r the giftie gie us
To see oursels as ithers see us!

Put in current English, '*May the Giver give his gift to us: to see ourselves as others see us!*'.

Our grandson, Vyāsa, a doctor in London, became a pet of the Boxall's. My wife, Andal and I, had called on them along with Vyāsa in 1980. The Boxall's virtually adopted him. Randolph passed away at the end of the century. Vyasa made it a point of calling on her in her loneliness. She fell ill and Vyasa shifted to look after her. Soon, there was no hope of her surviving. One evening, as my wife and I were talking after dinner, Vyasa telephoned. He said that he was sitting on her bed, with Mrs. Boxall's hand in his. She had wanted to say Goodbye to us. He held the telephone to her mouth, she said, "I wanted so much to talk to you. Goodbye." Vyasa, almost without a pause said, "She is breathing her last." "Wait," a moment later he said, "She is no more."

Vignette 9. *En route* to Alma Mater

Magdalen, Oxford

From the 10th year to the 17,[th] I had to satisfy my hunger for companions by companioning books. In Malaya, Singapore and even in the Wilderness School in Ashburton, Devon, S.W. England, where I was no ordinary Boarder but Parlour-Boarder in the Head Master's house. It was a peculiar home and not too pleasant despite companionship of an *ad hoc* sister, older than me by 3-years. She adopted me as another younger brother in preference to her own, younger by 4.I did not really have schoolmates with whom I would have normally associated. I did not have siblings. I realized my loss nearly 12-15 years later when children of my own, delightedly shared with me their childhood pranks and gambols.

I joined a Government School in Johore Bahru, capital of Johore, an Unfederated State in Malaya, in January 1930.I was 9 ½. It was opposite the north of Singapore Island, connected by a causeway. Our home was amid a 4-hectare grove of equatorial trees, fruit-bearing, coconut and rubber. My live companions were monkeys, squirrels and birds including cockatoos, parrots, pigeons and thrushes. Other children were a 20-minute walk away; Grandpa would not allow me out unless accompanied by himself! Books were the only alternative pastime. They were meant for English children. **Treasure Island, Kidnapped, Robinson Crusoe, Alice in Wonderland, Clive in India** (by Henty) and their like were bought for me by my father. We were chauffeur-driven to Singapore on Fridays, a holiday in Muslim Johore, mainly for my sake. Two books a week were the minimum; it went up at times to 4.Most were for over mid-teenage readers. Many happened to be published in Oxford. Some authors had Oxford degrees printed after their names. I decided to go to Oxford; to me it had become the Helicon, of European Wisdom. My two elders didn't seem to mind my spending more time with them, than on school books; nor did they care for examination marks. As it happened in my school, the English College, I had no fear of exams and marks were satisfactory.

I began to be spoilt by my first year's double promotion from Std. III to Std. V; then, after only 3 months, I was supposed to be too good for V; I was kicked upstairs to VI. By the end of 1931, I found myself in Std. VII, not yet having completed my 11th year. English College had a peculiar rule: those who were not as good in Mathematics as in all other subjects could be given special coaching in Mathematics separately. This enabled me to make up for my relatively average Math's as against excellence in Arts. I finished school with Senior Cambridge equivalent to the English O-Level, in December 1933. I could not be admitted into any English University without Latin for the Entrance Admission Examination in Arts. Therefore, I had to have private lessons, which I duly had. As I felt that I had a lot of spare time, I also studied, on my own, Roman and Greek History. I enjoyed Latin and loved History. They have remained my chief intellectual props to this very day, when, within 8-weeks, I shall be 93.

Weekly tuition in Latin was given by Mr. Tiddemann, apparently of German extraction, a teacher in the Raffles Institution. In the 11 months before the Senior Cambridge Examination, I managed to cover the entire course, both in Latin and Greco-Roman History. The three of us at home thought that I could be admitted into an English University straightway. It was not so. No further education was available in Singapore. Father, being a WOG, determined that I should go only to England. He contacted a school in England through the tourist agency Messrs. Thomas Cook and Son's branch in Singapore. He decided upon Wilderness School. I was to be a Parlour-Boarder, becoming part of the headmaster's family. He felt that I would be sufficiently anglicized there. Thank Heaven, he was wrong.

The Headmaster of Wilderness, Mr. Henry Naylor, wrote that it would be absolutely necessary for me to know French if I were to join Wilderness. I had my father's old copy of **Hugo's French Simplified**. It had 28 Lessons. As I was to travel by ship, the journey would take me 31 days. As there were only 28 lessons, I would have 3 days for revision. Mr. Hugo assured us on the first sentence of his booklet that the reader could teach himself. Furthermore, he would, within 6 months be able to make himself understood in Paris. Fortune smiled on me. In Wilderness, I got top marks in the Senior Cambridge Examination, including French! I took an Oxford Admission-Scholarship examination in August 1938 for entrance into College in October. I had finished my Higher Cambridge

School Certificate[14] with good enough marks to have the necessary qualifications for University Entrance. I was called for an interview in Magdalen in its President's Office. It was for any one of 3 colleges: Baliol, New College and Magdalen. I won no Scholarship but got Admission after Interview.

I presented myself punctually. The Interview was in Magdalen's great Dining Hall. On the other side of the High Table, slightly raised from the floor, with 3 high chairs next to the wall and a tripod in front, three gowned Dons were seated. I sat on the tripod. The President on the central chair told me that to his right was the Dean of Divinity, the Reverend Adam Fox, the Moral Tutor; to his left was the Tutor of English Language and Literature, Mr. C.S. Lewis. The President was Dr. Gordon who was also the Oxford University Professor of English Poetry. Mr. Lewis was also a University Professor. His lectures were always held in Magdalen Hall which used to be chock full with all students of English in the University and an equal number from other Faculties. Mr. Lewis was a distinguished medievalist and a humorous speaker.Rev. Adam Fox was to become, immediately I left Magdalen in 1941, the Dean of Westminster, London, the highest job in that Cathedral. (Please pardon this interlude; but it does tell you in what esteem both the College and the University, including their personnel, are held.)

President and Moral Tutor were audience, silent but most attentive. I bowed, and they bowed to me.

> C.S.Lewis: *Why do you choose English Language and Literature?*
>
> V.S. Charry: *I enjoy it. I want to teach it. I can't think of a better calling. I love Elizabethan and Jacobean Drama. Besides, one has to know English very well before one can specialize in Politics, Philosophy and Economics. (PPE[15])*
>
> CSL: *Hmm! What was the antecedent of **The Merchant of Venice**?*
>
> VSC: ***The Jew of Malta,** Barabas the usurer and prototype of Shylock, by Christopher Marlowe, whose "**Mighty line**" would be so useful to Shakespeare.*

---

[14] **HCSC:** *Equivalent to the Indian Pre-University Courses (Std. XII)*

[15] **PPE:** *Faculty of which the lectures I wished to attend when they didn't clash with my Faculty's.*

CSL: (*After looking at the smiling President). Hmm. Hmm. You have spoken a volume in a sentence. Thank you. You have read Shakespeare?*

VSC: *Through and through.*

CLS: *When?*

VSC: *July and August 1935. Aboard the good ship **Fushimi Maru** en route from Singapore to Tilbury in 31 days.*

CLS: ***Hamlet?***

VSC: *Of course,*

CSL: *Who says, "**Perpend**"?*

VSC: *Polonius, pompously asking the Queen, Hamlet's mother, to listen carefully about his daughter, Ophelia, having told him about Hamlet's attentions to her.*

CSL: (*to the President) I look forward to the privilege of being Mr. Charry's Tutor.*

President: *Congratulations, Mr. Charry. You shall hear from our Office. Good bye.*

VSC: *Thank you, Sirs.*

I bowed and retreated.

On the rare occasions when I spend a night in Oxford, the keeping of the hours by the clock towers in New College, and Merton, and the great booming of Tom tolling 101 times at 9 pm at Christ Church are inextricably interwoven with memories and regrets and lost joys. The sound almost sends me mad, so intense are the feelings it evokes.

A. N. Wilson

VIGNETTE 10. MAGDALEN

1938-1941

Oxford's Academic Year[16] always starts on the first Monday of October. My first term started in October 1938. War clouds were gathering. All, hoping that they would disperse, acted completely unaffected by the Future. Letters to and fro undergraduate and home became briefer and briefer, only because of lack of time. We had too many irons in the fire. Settling down itself was absolutely no problem because it was mechanical. Convention dominated. I had to take part in many things. I was asked to join Political Societies and couldn't resist. I became a life member of the Conservative because in some ways, it *conserved* my culture; I became College Secretary of the Liberals: I felt that one should be free and easy in Opinion; I attended some Labour Club meetings because my closest friends in Magdalen wanted to argue with me as an Indian. Likewise, with the Communist Club. Finally, there was the **Indian Majlis** of which I became a prime-mover and President in my last term. It played a crucial part in my life. In Games, I was pestered into joining the College hockey team simply because Indians were supposed to be magicians with the hockey stick; I soon proved to them that I was an exception and gave it up in favour of Squash. I was fond of water: I became a "Wet Bob," and was taken into the Rowing Club. Magdalen had its Houseboat moored against the **Isis'** bank; The Thames, which flows on to London, is called **Isis** in Oxford recalling Egypt where

---

[16] Oxfords **Academic Year** *always starts on first Monday's of the Christian calender in each of the three Terms of each 8 weeks: Hillary, Michaelmas and Easter. Each term lasts exactly eight weeks, totalling therefore 24 weeks in the year. Vacations are of 6 weeks each after Hillary and Michaelmas. After Easter come the summer holidays right up to October. All Terms start on Mondays. Unlike in many other parts of the world, these dates have been unchangeable for more than a thousand years.*

Isis was the **Nile's** chief Goddess who created the fertile and populous banks.

Within College were 2 important rooms; the Junior and the Senior Common Rooms respectively for undergraduates and graduates including the Dons, the colloquial term for the College's Teachers, including the President, though a rare visitor. The proper term is **Fellows.** The two rooms were certainly not common; I only entered the SCR once to handover a paper to my tutor.

The JCR was in the Cloisters, the chief and original quadrangle, on the first floor. Entrance was from the ground floor where, in a kitchenette, presided over by an ancient ex-member of the Helping Staff, one could get all kinds of drinks and miscellaneous articles. The Magdalen cellar was 100-feet long and 30 wide. It was supposed to be the best equipped cellar in England after those of the Monarch and the Inns of Court. Vintage Wine was completely swathed in spider-webs, decades old. Only a couple of undergraduates could afford even a single bottle. I managed to *see* one! JCR chairs were decades old and the more comfortable for that; had it not been for the closure of the JCR by 9:30 p.m., one would have gone off to sleep in one of them. Strangely, in my times at least, Cigar smoking was rife. Only with difficulty and loss of face, could one refuse to smoke "at least one fag, please."In Magdalen and in most Colleges one had to accept the precept: "When in Rome do as Romans do." It was, however, safe to pretend to do so, and get away with it. It made for tolerance and gentlemanliness.

My rooms were too expensive for me. I had to wait for the end of the Academic Year, June '39 to move into a more affordable one. My first was in the aristo-plutocratic St. Swithin's quadrangle immediately turning left from the main college entrance. I was in Swithin's VII/1. The drawing room was about 12 feet square; the bedroom about 12 by 6. Windows, looking on to the Long Wall Quad., were barred. I could squeeze myself in and out; but didn't do so after having proved to myself that I could if necessity arose.

Participation in Games was considered essential in all English Schools and Colleges. The most important Sports Event was the **Oxford and Cambridge Annual Boat Race;** so important that it took place neither in Oxford nor Cambridge but in London, capital of Britain itself on the Thames. Rowing was upstream. Thousands of onlookers lined both banks and crowded the boats moored along the shore. The Race, being near the Houses of Parliament, the Cabinet and many MP's were also spectators;

many of them had graduated from the two Universities. The Royal family too was represented sometimes by the Monarch. A tally of the Races from the last century up to the latest is jealously kept. All this made me accept the invitation to join the Magdalen Boat Club. I was light-weight and not too skilled an oarsman. I had sufficient know-how about currents in the river which were most changeable on the Isis. So I was, inevitably, a Cox; and fit enough for the Magdalen First Eight. Magdalen was often the Head of the River (Isis).As Rowing was King of all Ox-Cam sports, my lot was prestigious: I was a Wet-Bob, not a mere Dry-Bob. This counted in England as the supreme qualification for any aspirant for any job. One had to take care not to forget to mention it in any Application. I didn't forget. My first Application was also the last.

The Oxford Majlis was founded in the early 20th century. It was called **Majlis** recalling the Persian (Iranian) Parliament. Why Persian? It had been the accepted court language under the Mughals, and even the Peshwas of Pune (formerly Poona) used in communication not only with Delhi but in their own territory. My paternal grandfather learnt Persian when he was posted in Hyderabad. In the beginning, the Majlis members belonged to all the Countries of the British Empire in South and South East Asia. A Ceylonese (now Sri Lankan), was one of its earlier Presidents, Solomon Bandaranayake. When I was posted in Colombo in 1951 he was a Minister in the first Ceylonese Cabinet. When I told him that I had been one of his successor Presidents of the Majlis, it immediately made me one of his favourite and genuine friends; Oxford has its uses. The Majlis was restricted to Indians after India's Independence.

One Indian student in Oxford was a fellow student for a year. Despite earnest endeavours, the then Majlis President could not persuade her to join. She avoided all Indian company. She was in Somerville College for only one year and kept only European company. I saw her once leaving the theatre after the show accompanied by, of course, a non-Indian. After 25 years, I met her again in company with her father, Jawaharlal Nehru, who was visiting Peking, China. Her name was Indira Gandhi, wife of Feroze Gandhi, a Parsee.

A complete contrast was Vengalil Krishnan **Krishna Menon** (VKKM). Except for a few aiming at British Indian Government Services, all Oxonian Indians became fans of VKKM.Every Majlis President invariably visited him in London and hosted him in Oxford. He spoke regularly to us, promoting India's demand for Independence. He was an inexpensive guest, quite content with unlimited cups of tea and a morsel of food in Oxford's only Indian Restaurant, the Taj Mahal. We both became really close to each other. It is not surprising that it didn't take him long to know about my participation in the Oxford Union debate on Indian Independence. That took me even closer to him which was of utmost help in my Bombay posting when I dealt with Goa (*vide. Vignette Nos., 41-44*).

Two Magdalen alumni were of great interest to me: one was Wolsey who became a Cardinal and Henry VIII's right hand man. He founded another college, Christ Church; the biggest in Oxford called **The House** by Oxonians. Wolsey was a brilliant Latin Scholar. Both Oxford and Cambridge Universities were founded by the Roman Catholic Church primarily to produce Priests. This practice was modified automatically when Henry VIII broke away from the Roman Catholic Church and, virtually (or viciously) made himself the Pope and appointed the two leaders of the Anglican Catholic Church: Archbishops of Canterbury and York; the former being senior. "Pope" Henry VIII was no authority on the Bible and may have read little of it after his childhood. Significantly, the word *Catholic* was retained. The reformation in N.W. Europe made many English Christians try to reform the Anglican Catholic Church. Wolsey was much criticized for his being too Catholic, and conserving the power of the Church over in its flock in "Pope" Henry VIII. However, his fall was due to Henry having an affair with Anne Boleyn, a Lady-in-Waiting of his Queen, Catharine, sister of King Philip of Spain. Henry had sent Wolsey to the Pope in Italy to have his first marriage annulled both because he was fed up with Catharine and Anne had conceived. The unfortunate Pope (and more unfortunate Wolsey) could not oblige Henry, at any cost. The Pope was virtually prisoner in Naples of King Philip. Henry made Wolsey and his successors reduce all revenues in property and privileges of the English ecclesiastics; he needed money to finance ruinous Wars across the English channel. Wolsey would have been executed for treason, but he avoided the Block in the Tower of London by succumbing to disease in good time. Anne was the mother of Queen Elizabeth-I. She was executed because she had an affair with a Courtier.

Oscar Wilde was my other hero. Freshers covet his room. All students make it a point of becoming a guest of the lucky occupant. As dramatists of relatively modern English comedy, I appreciate most Oscar Wilde coupled with Bernard Shaw. Wilde scaled to the top of his profession and like Wolsey came to an unhappy end as an exile in France.

No Oxonian or Cantabrian can forget his Scout. He is your Jeeves, the valet who looks after you, your room, belongings and behaviour[17]. My Longwall Annex accommodation consisted of the drawing room and a separate bedroom. The window of drawing room framed the lovely Magdalen Tower, to me the most lovely in the world. It welcomes all who come to Oxford from London, Magdalen being the first College to the right after passing the beautiful bridge over Cherwell which flows through Magdalen grounds with its own with a beautiful path right round it and a culvert leading to the New Buildings (built about 250 years ago!). This path is Addison's Walk commemorating the great writer of the early 18th century. Magdalen Tower was greeted by me every morning as I prayed, looking as eastward as possible. It is Oxford's tallest Tower, and in my time, tallest building in Oxford. It is 140 feet high. A hundred of us would be invited to climb up to its top on May Day, now observed as Labour Day. We sang songs as musically as we could to greet the "Merry Month." Our Tower would shake a little beneath us when we sang, no doubt expressing its admiration. Some fellow undergraduates wouldn't appreciate that at all: they felt sea-sick. I had been a good Able Bodied sailor, and so hoisted myself up every one of the 3 years I was there: an unforgettable experience.

The greatest gift that Oxford gives her sons is,
I truly believe, a genial irreverence toward learning,
and from that irreverence love may spring.

Robertson Davies

---

[17]   **Behaviour**: *This appertains mainly to ethical matters about which the Moral Tutor is informed. An important caveat is that bedrooms should not be entered by any guest, male or female. Breaking Bounds means going out of and, of course, also climbing back out of hours. i.e., 11 pm and 6 am. Legitimate exit may only be effected through the main entrance, the Porter's Lodge, even that with prior notice and agreement of the Moral Tutor.*

Vignette 11. Ox-Cam Scout

Let's get back to Messenger, my first Scout.

I had two Jeeves: Messenger in my first year in the posh Swithin's Quad VII/1 room and the other, Bolton, in the much cheaper Magdalen Annex, separated from the College by Long Wall road. My rooms were on the second floor. Bolton was much younger. He was my Scout for two years after which both of us left Oxford. He was conscripted for the War. I returned to India by ship on, a 100-day voyage round the Cape of Good Hope.

"Scout," nowadays, brings to mind Baden Powell's Boy Scouts and his and his sister's Girl Guides. Both have become Institutions in schools in many English-speaking countries, and even in a few speaking other languages. Boy Scouts and Girl Guides came into being in 1908 and 1910 respectively. They are estimated to be now 25-million strong. The word *scout* itself is Germanic; as a verb, it conveys, predicatively, "searching" or "looking for," as used in: "*I scouted all over* the shop to find a fishing rod; but didn't succeed." Powell's *Scout* was derived from an Army infantry term: a soldier in uniform but unarmed whose duty was to reconnoiter enemy's side of the battle field, usually at night and before Action began. A scout had to obtain information about the enemy's numbers, dispositions, and possible. According to International Law, a captured Scout was treated on the same basis as any soldier in proper uniform. Although he had spied, he was unarmed and so, not a killer. Therefore, he was treated as a surrendering enemy soldier. Baden Powell had been in the British Army and served in various countries including India. His chief feats took place in South Africa in the war with the **Boers, the** South African Dutch. This happened early in the 20th century. The war was extremely tough because of the Boer's tremendous courage and tactics. Although they lost the war, the English had to compromise because the Boers were a great majority beyond the Vaal River in Transvaal and Orange Free State. Because of their guerrilla tactics, the British had to copy them. Scouts played a great part on both sides. Not only courage but the ability to cope with the unexpected was essential.

Scouts had to know First Aid, knotting ropes and strings, making fires, camping huts, swimming, direction finding through compasses and telescopes, cooking, sowing and even whistling in various notes and pitches. That is why Scouting and Guiding are so popular with children and youth. This rather lengthy introduction may help to describe some of the qualities of the Ox-Cam Scout.

Mr. Messenger, my first Scout in Magdalen introduced himself to me in my room, which he had opened for me, with: *"Mornin' Sir, I'm Messenger. Yer Scout. And yeu know wha' that means? I'm a Spy. But I spy for yer good. I go back an tell yer Moral Tutor all about yer, good and bad. So if you wonder why he' knows so much about yer, it's me who's spilt the beans."*

In the dictionaries, *Scout* is defined as man's servant. It would be politer to call him a Valet. In the Universities, however, they are referred to as: "my Jeeves," the great character invented by Wodehouse to be the friend, philosopher and guide of Berty Wooster. In Magdalen however, we might refer to him as **Lane, Jack's** valet in **Importance of being Earnest** by Oscar Wilde, who graduated from Magdalen.

I replied to Messenger in my own English:*"Thank you, Mr. Messenger."* He interrupted: *"Nay Mister, I'm only Messenger."*He resumed his advice with "Don'ts"

Don't break bounds! = don't try to get over the walls and risk life and limb as well as being sent "down" = expelled

Don't have girls outside hours = only between 4 p.m. and 6:30.

Don't be late for lunch and dinner = Enter before 1:15pm and 7:14 p.m.

Don't miss breakfast = between 8 a.m. and 8:45

Don't go to dinner or lecture without your gowns (At the end of 3 years, we are not in gowns but in rags, gowns having been used even for cleaning up of spilt coffee and shoes at times)

Don't ever enter the lecture room after the lecture starts or leave before it ends. (All lectures started on the hour at 10 a.m. and lasted for 45 minutes, (thus enabling you to cycle madly to the next which may be anything up to 2 miles within 10 minutes). Pinching a cycle within your college costs you a mug of beer to the owner. Pinching it outside a lecture hall costs you a minimum of £5—if you are caught.)

Don't fall ill without my permission (If I sneezed, Messenger would come to know it and try to give First Aid.)

Don't forget the tip at the end of the each term. You'll know why, when you've done so! I never knew because I never forgot.

Messenger was quite an old man; I guess about 55 and took to me most affectionately. He was too old to be conscripted for the War. However, I shifted rooms, and so said goodbye to him and started off with Bolton. My tips to Messenger were £5 at the end of each term, without fail. Actually, I saved lot of money in 2nd and 3rd terms even more than I had done in the 1st. The mystery is that Messenger served all the staircases in Swithin's and therefore, some 21 undergraduates, most of whom were extremely wealthy. They gave many extravagant parties almost every week and ordered for more food and drink than necessary, despite Messenger telling them not to waste money. His revenge was to help himself to left over's, and generously complement my parties which would have been Spartan otherwise.

Bolton was quite different from Messenger but equally solicitous of my welfare. He didn't lecture me, as I was no longer a Fresher. We liked each other a lot and neither us had any complaints whatever. His reports about me to my Reverend Moral Tutor were not as lengthy as Messenger's had been. By my 2nd year onwards the Reverend Adam Fox was my host for supper once in every 4 weeks. Incidentally, my tip to Bolton, considered quite satisfactory as a junior scout's, was only £2 a term.

Ox-Cam Scouts have a share in the upbringing of undergraduates which can't be underestimated. Not only are the Don'ts important, many Do's were timely. They included time-tabling of days' routines, looking after one's clothes; most important in Oxford, seeing to the top condition of one's bicycle. In my case, this last was most helpful: because all my travel yearly of a 1000-miles if not more every year, was vital to my getting to know my environment which moulded me into a hardy "Annual" at almost no cost of travel.

Vignette 12. Vacations

Youth Hostelling In England

1939-'41

    The real vacation in England is when many other fellowmen and women are also enjoying themselves in summer. It was a fine opportunity for me to be with all kinds of people, called 'ordinary' men but each of them with that variation of character, apart from looks, which makes an alien feel really at home. For undergraduates like me in Oxford, it was a treat. Magdalen, my college and my home for 3 years, was not the same from July to September. Almost everyone deserted it. There would be more strangers, tourists, than anyone who "belonged." There would not even be the regular chief porter at the gate but an unhappy substitute who forewent one month of his vacation to be on duty. His only consolation may have been extra pay. I could not remain in college because even my scout would be away, the kitchen would be closed and the Junior Common Room locked. The grounds, empty of college mates and absence of their laughter, were forbidding. The answer was to see a little more of England and the English. I did. That too was real Education. As I was not affluent, I did not waste any cash on visits to Paris, or the Riviera as many of my Indian fellow undergraduates could afford to do even though they knew no French to be able to get to know the French. What's the good of going to a country and not getting to know its people?

    The leanness of my purse was an incentive. I am grateful for it. I had my lovely, aero plane-metal (duraluminium) horse with 3 gears. I could lift her with the little finger of my left hand, my faithful bicycle. She never let me down; never had a puncture in her 3 year attachment to me. She had a metal tray-like thing behind the seat on which someone else could sit. It carried my rucksack with all I needed for my "sen'night

Anabasis[18]." I became member of the Youth Hostel Association (YHA) for the princely sum of £1 per annum. It enabled me to spend a night or two in any of the Youth Hostels all over the country for a shilling a night. (1£ = 20 shillings, = Rs.13·4). This meant that I spent only 75 paise per night, in today's money, virtually nothing! I lived on buns, milk and fruit with a bit of cheese. All that cost me about 2 ½ shillings, not even Rs. 2.

My rucksack also carried a thin sleeping-bag with a fold to permit a pillow to be put inside below the head. Youth Hostels were in 2 sections, for males and females respectively, separated by the wardens' suites. There was electric light but no plugs. Water closets had no wash basins. There were half a dozen outside in each section in the corridors. Couples were parted for the nights; a good thing. Members could not check in before 6 p.m. and had to check out by 6:30 a.m. making outdoor life compulsory, fair or foul, rain or sun. There were no bathrooms. This didn't matter to the natives. I had my baths and washed my jersey and unmentionables in any stream that bubbled past the roads. I cycled on. Sometimes, though rarely, I used to doze away for half an hour after the washing, bath and lunch on buttered buns and cheese. I carried the butter in the rucksack, my *akshayapāthram*, cornucopia. A cup of milk was usually given to me by the farmer's wife whose farm was along the roadside. I never succeeded in paying for the milk because: **a)** I was an Indian, and so a rare bird; **b)** I cycled; **c)** I had my Magdalen hockey jersey on me: the English loved a sportsman.—I confess I had no right to the shirt as I had been dropped from the team; **d)** At the good lady's request I gave short oral biography of myself; and **e)** She called her children to see the specimen of an Indian. To my embarrassment the daughters, when they were there, loudly whispered flattering things about the Indian animal who had escaped from the zoo. Some farmer's wives were so generous as to ask me to stay on for 'dinner'—as lunch is called in the English countryside—so that I could be shown off to Daddy (the master of the house). I politely declined as I had to reach my destined hostel in time and so could not linger. All this was delighting education. I realized how barbarous urban "civilization" was as against primaevality.

Apart from landscapes and even the actual cycling, I became a collector of cathedrals, monuments, centuries old dwelling houses,

---

[18] ***Anabasis***: *meaning **journey** in Greek. It is the name of a classic on the retreat of Greek soldiers from Iraq back to Greece led by Xenophon their commander.*

manors, and a variety of what we would call bazaars. It was good that I could afford no camera: all I saw are vivid to me in remembrance. I can't lose the images, neither can they fade till I am no more to see them.

I had a one-inch-to-the-mile map as my guide. I peddled about 40 **km** a day, spending nights in alternate Hostels reaching usually by dusk, about 7 p.m. In Youth Hostels, we had to check in and take out from an urn, job-tickets, allotting the type of work to be done. I think I got, during all my cycle tours, every one of the possible tasks. There were nearly almost a dozen: sweeping; cleaning dining room tables; washing and drying dishes; cleaning lavatories, going to nearest shops to get vegetables, eggs, bread and so forth and, if competent, cooking. There were 2 urns of different colours with job tickets also of different colours, one for males and one for females. Normally, if there were equal numbers of males and females, as they were frequently, each male could have a female comrade for the same task. Couples could also exchange the tasks. The warden wouldn't be visible after 8 p.m. He switched lights off at 10 and disappeared till 6 a.m. Altogether, every YHA member found himself or herself meeting every kind of person with varied callings: cab drivers, students, painters, jugglers, gymnasts, factory workers, shop-personnel, sailors, and the even un-uniformed soldiers. I felt as though I had the whole variety of humanity around me. We were united I think by Mother Nature. My being there obviously made my fellow travelers the happier for having a non-English colleague and, even better, a non-European. Not for a moment did I feel that I was an unwanted stranger. Not one Youth Hosteller attempted to be superior to another. Youth Hostelling, as it was in England, proved that *"Round the Four Seas, all Men are Brothers"*, (title of a Chinese classic). I would perhaps, for the Youth Hostels, alter the motto to *"Round the Four Seas all are Brothers and Sisters"*.

My longest cycling trip covered 200kms, 6:30 a.m. to 7:30 p.m. from Oxford to Exeter with no sight-seeing *en route*. I had to keep an appointment. Unsurprisingly I was exhausted. My trips covered Wales from North to South over the heights of Rhayader and then over to Tintern and Bristol. Being amid the contrasts was thrilling. The voices of the Welsh in their Churches were exalting. When I got back to Oxford and talked about my travels to fellow undergrad Indians, I never succeeded in persuading a single one of them to join me in future trips. When I was a Diplomat, all English colleagues in the Corps became close friends because of my love for the ordinary people of England and having seen more of their own country than they themselves had done. Throughout my career, my Youth Hostelling was my guide. In every country where I was posted, except of course, Hong Kong and Singapore, my wife accompanied me specifically to see and meet as many people of different regions as possible. I concluded that most people who had "little learning" would have been better without any. It applies particularly to India. As in the past, India would be a happier and richer country economically, as it actually was till 1870[19] if schooling ended for 90% by teenage.

---

[19]   **1870**: *The authority for this statement was the London Economist, I think, of March 1912.*

MARRIAGE—A LA BRĀHMANIQUE

Vignette 13. Espousal-I

Pourparlers

I returned from England, aged 21; still a bachelor! I loved teaching and children. I enjoyed life despite almost 16 hours of work daily, Monday to Saturday. Yet there was something missing. Being exhausted, I had no time to guess the answer and cater to the need.

Dehra Dun was less than an hour away by train from Hardwar (or Hari-Dwara, meaning the Portal to Divinity), on the banks of the holy Ganga. It was pleasant to wash off one's sins once a week in early spring and summer. The holiest spot in which to bathe was, in local parlance, Har-ki-paudi, the foot-print of Vishnu in the bed of the Ganga. Some evenings, and always before dawn they were no crowds there. I left Dehra Dun on Saturdays by train in the cheapest class before sunset. To and fro, it cost Rs. 2. As I had Rs. 200 a month and spent only ten on bearer (my Indian scout) and monthly tea, all other necessities being free, I could enjoy the outing. At Hardwar too, there was hardly ever any expenditure except on a meal. After some time even this expenditure was not needed. Rs. 8 monthly, to and fro to Hardwar was good investment to wash off sins accumulated every week, wasn't it? I started these little pilgrimages in March '42, and the sin load was not too heavy to carry.

The cool rushing water that Mother Ganga poured over her child rubbed off even the thin layer of intention to sin. It was heavenly. As my Saturday pilgrimages were uninterrupted, an elderly gentleman found me a constant fellow traveler. We both took shelter on Saturday nights in the only South Indian Dharma Shāla[20] which welcomes Brāhmaṇas by allotting an exclusive hall for their sojourn and meditation. My fellow companion was a Mr. Harihar Iyer. We lay each on a mat next to each other. Being an elder, I always greeted him first with folded hands. One

---

[20] *Free accommodation setup by Trusts for Hindu pilgrims.*

day I actually did *Shastanga Namaskara*[21] , it being our Solar New Year's day. Like all native Indians, the younger had to disclose all vital statistics to the elder. These included: Name, Gothra, Dharma and minor matters like job, pay, hometown, age, and gradually all details of family members of up to two generations backwards (if you knew them). On his own, but according to custom he disclosed to me that he was a Palghat (Kerala) Brāhmanā and in service with the Government's Geological Survey of India, in Dehra Dun. After a couple of months, our acquaintance deepened. I was invited for lunch every Sunday in his home, in Dehra Dun. In the Dharma Shala too, he ordered dinners for us both, insisting on paying. His family consisted of 2 daughters and 3 sons. The eldest, a son, was 2 years younger than me. My having become a regular "Week-Boy," I was an accepted member of the family. Indeed, it was not possible to escape because, we returned from Hardwar by the same train and was compelled to accompany him in the same tonga to his residence.

Shree Iyer, having discovered everything necessary about me, felt it was his duty to advise me about my future. My qualifications, he deemed, were too high to teach in a mere School, however famous and well paid. I should, therefore, aim at a University post and rise to be at least head of a college, if not University Vice-Chancellor, even as my grandfather had risen to the dizzy height of the topmost native in the British Indian Army Audits and Accounts. It would have been impolite of me to argue the point with him. One day, he informed me that he had written to his close friend in Bangalore, Chief Secretary of Mysore State, of which the Maharaja was the great Krishna Devaraja Wadiyar. Mysore, his State, was actually the best part of India. He told me that his friend had replied to advise me to call on him in Bangalore at his residence on my next vacation (in July).Though I was not keen, it was only polite for me to do so, and so I did. He was Mrry[22]. Sri. B.T. Keshava Iyengar (BTK). His residence was in Basavangudi, Bangalore, where I used to stay with

---

[21] *Complete prostration on the floor being touched by 6 points (1. palms held out together, 2.forehead, 3. nose, 4. the navel, and 5 and 6. toes of each foot kept together), a prime Yogic posture. When one does shastanga namaskara, one says in the pravara, what ones's gothra is. The* **pravara** *is the announcement of personal particulars to priests and elders, said ritually.*

[22] **Maharajasreegal**, *a respectful form of address equivalent to the English Rt. Hon'ble.*

my aunt and her husband, Sri Kuppuswamy Iyengar (CSK), a short walk away from BTKs home.

I was received not merely politely but affectionately. Sri BTK was simply dressed in a Dhoti.[23] He told me that he would give me a letter to the Vice-Chancellor of Mysore University, Sri M. Subba Rao who would duly advise me. Casually, Sri BTK told me that my aunt's husband was one of his closest friends and a colleague in Mysore Government Service. Sri CSK's wife was my aunt Manjulmma, my mother's second younger sister. I always stayed with them for a part of my vacations. When I returned, Manjula Chitti[24] started smiling and asked me about the interview and whether I had seen any other member of the family. Innocently I told her that a girl had brought coffee for me. Chitti asked me what she looked like. I said, I didn't take note of her, Chitti left it at that.

I did go to Mysore and met the Vice-Chancellor. He asked me about my career and emoluments and perks in Doon School. After hearing the details, he told me that it was unthinkable for me to accept a mere lecturer ship which is all that might be available to me at Rs. 150 monthly, with no perks, accommodation or allowances. Furthermore, it was not advisable for me as a Brāhmanā to join the University. Brāhmanās were not welcome; they were already too many of them. Besides, I would remain as mere lecturer for decades and perhaps be superseded. I was delighted and thanked him sincerely.

---

[23] **Dhoti.** *The nether garment of a male adult, 4½ yds. long and 2½ wide, usually of cotton and sometimes silk, preferably handmade. The female equivalent is the* **Saree, and** *six yds. long and 2½ wide.*

[24] **Chitti.** *In Tamil all one's mother's younger sister or sisters. Mother's elder sisters are called as Peri-amma. Male counterparts are, peri-appa for uncle's order than one's father (appa), and chit-appa for his younger brothers.*

Vignette 14. Espousal-II

Iyengar Wedding

I duly called on Sri. Keshava Iyengar (BTK) to tell him what had transpired in Mysore University. The Vice-Chancellor had already written to him about his advice. Sri. BTK then said that he had spoken to my aunt's husband, Sri.CSK, about another matter; he would no doubt tell me about it. Even before Sri.CSK could tell me anything, Manjula Chitti, being a woman, couldn't help divulging the subject. It was a marriage proposal from Sri. BTK. Chitti asked me whether I wished to be married. Without beating about the bush, I said, "Yes."What kind of a girl would I like to marry? Answer: one of my own colour; of course, shorter than me; as young as possible; lively and even a bit of a tom-boy. She should be able to cook *Shātamadu*[25]. Chitti: "I think I've found your dream girl." Within a couple of days, I had to leave for Dehra Dun to be in time for the next Term.

Brāhmanā *Vadagalai*[26], Vaishnavite[27] Iyengar[28] sects are flexible as to ritual but Vedantically exacting and precise about Marriage itself. Ritual is determined by usage and tradition. They are meant for the public. Weddings are reasons for the extended family to meet under the patronage and expense of the bride's family. The bridegroom and party used to be accommodated nearby for a sojourn of at least 3 to 5 days. Nowadays, 24 hours is the limit.

---

[25]   *Shātamadu:* it is commonly known as **Mulligatawny,** (pepper water) in English. There are many kinds, commonly called **Rasam** (juice).However, the Iyengar specimen is unique. I call it **Brown-Label Iyengar Whiskey,**though non-alcoholic.

[26]   *Vadagalai.* A Tamil word meaning Northerner. (see also Vignette no. 50)

[27]   *Vaishvanite. Worshippers of Vishnu.*

[28]   *Iyengar.* Honorific given normally for any person, but now restricted to Viashnavites, spelt variously in English, and a caste designation.

Rituals vary, and are of secondary importance, provided the 5 main rites are duly performed: a. formal reception of bridegroom and party, the former arriving in horse carriage, accompanied, sometimes, by his eldest lady relative, and, obligatorily, at least one child of his extended family; b. the bride is kept out of sight, by close relatives, signifying that they approve of each other after seeing each other for the first time; holding a richly woven curtain and lowered after prayers; c. the bride and groom exchange garlands 3 times, the latter beginning the show; d. tying of the golden token of Marriage, the *Māngalyam*[29] by the bridegroom round the neck of the bride with 3 knots symbolizing the strength of Marriage; e. *Sapthapadi (seven steps)* of circumambulating clockwise the Holy Fire, readied for the prescribed Vedic prayers. There are other features which are part of the gaiety such as looking for the star, *Arundathi*, (constant wife) in the Great Bear, *Saptha Rushi (Seven Seers);* the bride crossing the threshold of the entrance door of where husband and party are accommodated.

Throughout the wedding a great deal of music, traditionally is provided by *Mangalavādu (*Happiness Bringers), actually barbers by profession. They play *volga,* oboe-like wind instruments from dawn to at least till lunch. At the *Mangalyam* time, they play *fortissimo,* accompanied, as always by *mrindaga* (drums) to make everyone stand and sprinkle *akshatẽ* (rice, yellowed with *manjal* and *kumkuma,* turmeric and saffron) over the married couple. Surprisingly, to foreigners, the couple don't drive away with shoes, usually thrown at them. Indeed, the bride is so young that she continues to live with her parents for a while before she joins her husband. She will be busy preparing to learn to manage her household according to the whims of her husband's family which will be subtly ascertained. The subtlety is again managed by the barber. He used to go to every house in the area every day, not only to shave the adult males, but also to collect a fund of information about everybody. When 'Mr. Gillette' took away his job of daily shaving, his wife substituted. She took whatever was necessary for the ladies' beautification and even medicines. It may be recalled that barbers in the Middle Ages everywhere were virtually also doctors, clipping nails being one of the operations they performed. The Middle Ages have still not vanished in India.

---

[29] **Mangalyam**: *a golden threaded token, never to be removed from the neck. Later it may be put on a golden necklace. The thread is dipped in saffron.*

Marriage *chez nous,* in its spiritual aspects, is rigidly Vedantic. It stems from happy experience of 3 millennia. It is beneficial. The fundamental purpose of marriage is that it is the first step in the Path of Evolution: the infinitesimal *Jeevātma's* (Soul) purpose is perpetual merger into Infinite Divinity; the two becoming One, *Advaita.* Brāhmanic worship enjoins both husband and wife to be together at least once daily. This togetherness is what is sought when the infinitesimal becomes part of the whole. Both Vedantically and logically, it infers that even in reincarnation, they are inseparable. The Ego vanishes. Similarly, husband and wife, ideally, do not remain egotistic *vis-ă-vis* each other. I becomes We. Hence, no truly Brāhmanic Vedantic marriage can be annulled. It is training for walking the Path of Life. Hence, any so called Legal Separation or Divorce is Spiritually irrelevant and sheer folly.

The second purpose is basically Social Welfare. Procreation is a duty. Chastity is mandatory. Progeny should be carefully nurtured in Spartan style; should not be over-indulged but taught how to live economically and dedicate oneself to the Supreme Goal, merger into ALL. Happiness, not transient pleasures, must be sought.

The third injunction, to both boys and girls, is to respect their ancestors to whom they owe their genes. In India, it starts with love for their parents. Sinic (Chinese) ancestor worship, as interpreted by Confucius and Mencius and recommended by them, was identical with Indic Vedantic practice. The difference in theory is that the Chinese were pragmatic rather than idealistic; they were not sure as to whether there is a such a thing as Divinity. Yet, to insure themselves, if their ancestors were really immortal, they would be keener to help their progeny, if need be by approaching God should there be one besides the gods of Nature, such as Air, Water and the Earth, the Sun and Stars.

Our wedding was meticulously performed on 31st August 1944. A couple of days later, I left for Dehra Dun again. My bride and her parents left for Rewa, capital of an Indian princely state some 20-miles south of Allahabad. Her father had retired from Mysore State Service and become the Revenue Minister of Rewa, a State like Mysore, but smaller. Its capital also called Rewa. It was far more primeval than Mysore and as attractive. As customary for a son-in-law, I was asked to spend my first Deepavali (Festival of Lights) in Rewa, after which I could take my bride with me. Naturally our departure, after joyful celebration, was regretted by all, including myself. However, we two were at last, and for the first time, alone with each other. Our honeymoon had started. We were soon in our bungalow in the Doon School. Till her arrival I had remained in the bachelor suite in Jaipur House.

The reception of the newly married couple in the Doon School was delightful. We enjoyed lavish hospitality, most affectionately given by every one of my Teacher colleagues and Helping Staff. The Head Master, Mr. Foot and his wife were most parental. Yet, we were still nostalgic about Rewa. It is famous for its White Tigers. Suitable for honeymooners, it was romantic not only with tigers, crocodiles, cobras, waterfalls and above all, folk who proved how much better it is to be Primaeval[30] than "Progressive."

> *Happy is the man who finds a true friend,*
> *and far happier is he who finds*
> *that true friend in his wife.*
>
> *Franz Schubert*

---

[30] ***Primaeaval:*** *literally,* **First Age**, *ancient Greeks and Romans called their first Age the Golden. In Sanskrit the first Age is known as* **Satya Yuga,** *(Age of Truth). Our contemporary Age is actually on its last legs. In this fourth age,* **Kaliyuga** *is in its last quarter, and I feel that it is ending soon: everything is progressively going wrong especially human character becoming worse and worse. As Oliver Goldsmith put it, in his* **Deserted Village** *"Ill fares the land to hastening ills a prey, Where Wealth accumulates and Men decay." Hopefully, Women don't. More hopefully,* **Satya Yuga** *is coming back.*

BACK TO INDIA IN WARTIME

Vignette 15. Voyage-III A

Glasgow to Freetown

August–November 42

World War II was intensifying. Britain's Army was evacuated after many casualties from northwest France. Several thousand tonnes of Allied shipping had been victims of the Luftwaffe (German Air Force) and the U-Boats (submarines). Allied fleets, supposed not to be carrying war material, and personnel and their convoys, tended to skirt neutral shores, just keeping out of their territorial waters, usually about 3 miles. International laws are intended to protect civilians and civilian craft. Actually, however, these laws are not always obeyed. My 100-day voyage started on 19th August 1942. I finally disembarked in Colombo on 29th November.

After having taken my B.A (Hons.), Degree in July 1942 when I was 22, India Office, London, did me the favour of finding a berth for me on the City of Hong Kong (**C of HK**) of Ellerman and Bucknall Line, its burthen about 9000 tonnes; an average vessel. Hopefully, she would reach me to Kolkatta (Calcutta). My ticket cost £ 90. I was in the lower berth of a 4-berth cabin on the corridor side, opposite the porthole side beside the sea. All 4 of us were Indians. Altogether there were 19 Indians on board. I was the youngest; the oldest being about 45. One Indian was actually Eurasian although he called himself Anglo-Indian. He was a cadet of the British Indian Army. Though in civilian clothes, he was taciturn and would hardly greet us. Others were a jolly lot and felt sorry for him. Unfortunately, he had a nasty fight with the only Pathan among us. He had called us "You natives . . . ." The Pathan caught hold of him by the scruff of his neck, lifted him over the railings, and shouted into his ear, "Will you apologize?" "Sorry," he muttered. The Pathan brought him back on the deck: "Now apologize to all of them?" He did.

Wartime Regulations forbade the discloser of Route. Even captains wouldn't know because we were in a convoy, eventually of 47 ships a few days after leaving Glasgow. We were guarded by 4 fast Destroyers. They circumnavigated our convoy at a tremendous speed. Convoys' speed is that of its slowest ship; we made, at most and in good weather, only about 8 knots an hour. The Destroyers had to see that one of them was always at the prow[31], (the front part or beak of a ship) another at centre of starboard, another directly behind the stern and the 4th on the larboard centre. Hence the Destroyers went at least double the speed of the convoy. Altogether, we encountered fair weather. It being summer and autumn, it was pleasant. One of us had a small compass; we were enabled to know at least which direction the convoy was wending its way. The convoy's Captains depended upon directions signaled by the leading Destroyer's Captain. Circumstances determined the route which had, therefore, to be flexible. We had till the end of September a slow but enjoyable trip. We went along, but never trespassed into the territorial waters of: Iceland, Greenland, Newfoundland, east USA from Maine to Florida, alongside Cuba and adjacent Caribbean Sea Islands, the Guiana's (British, Dutch and French), down the Brazilian coast up to the Cabo da San Roc, north of the estuary of the Amazon river. We had gone south east, and up to San Roc then proceeded directly east in the Waist[32] of the Atlantic between (narrowest stretch Brazil and West Africa).

It would have been unrealistic and loss of experience not to have had a storm! Twenty four hours after seeing Cabo da San Roc, we had the Mother of all Storms. Fasten your seat belts. The Mother started in the night and went on for over 24 hours. Decks emptied. Passengers gradually all (except me) confined themselves into their berths, fastened all the belts they had. Each had two. Lying in the berth, the ship heeled to starboard, you almost slept on the railing; then her prow went down you almost stood looking at your feet; she heeled larboard, you are almost lying on the steel wall on the left, then her stern went down to kiss the ocean, your feet is looking at your head. It is quite pleasant if you are a good sailor. Ninety nine per cent of the voyagers were not. They were busy emptying their insides. The dining saloon was empty, but for the

---

[31] *Prow, starboard, stern and larboard: front, right side, back and left side respectively.*

[32] *Waist of the Atlantic: the narrowest stretch of the Atlantic. This was done to avoid being targets of the U-Boats Prow, starboard, stern and larboard: front, right side, back and left side respectively.*

Captain and his right hand fellow-diner, myself. I had coxed Magdalen's First Boat in the Eights for three years and had full experience of currents. Besides, this was my 3rd voyage, not counting a day-trip from Southampton to Cherbourg on the **Normandie** (80,000 tonnes), and back a month later back to Southampton on the **Champlain** (30,000 tonnes), both of the French National Transatlantic Passenger line. The two ships, I was unhappy to learn, were lost later during the war; the Normandie having caught fire near New York and the Champlain was torpedoed by a U-Boat.

I confess that while I wasn't sea-sick, getting out of the dining saloon, I stumbled on the high threshold and cut my lower lip; this is my memento of Mother Storm. I have the stitches to prove it. All had recovered, in a day or two. We were supposed to be nearing safety as the convoy was sailing due East, we deduced that we were bound for Freetown, Sierra Leone, still a British possession. All French West Africa had fallen to the Axis[33].Our ships were short of water and perhaps also of fuel. We had to get the nearest port available. Even potable water wasn't there; we survived on wine (*gratis*); for baths we had salt water. Fortunately, there was sufficient wine. Within 18 hours we should have reached Freetown. One of us Indians had a *Panchanga* (almanac). He informed us that it was Deepāwali (festival of Garlands of Light). It is the most enjoyable pan-Indian fête. We had had our sumptuous dinner and were lolling on the front hatch-board covers. Being *amāvāsya* (New-Moon night), the stars shone brightly. One of our party was playing his flute; needless to say he was a Bengali. The whole sky lit up! Deepāwali!! No, Very Lights[34]created each a ten-second daylight discovering our entire fleet.

Then followed tremendous explosions. The foremost Destroyer was destroyed; 5 minutes later another; and then another; all 4 Destroyers gone. The convoys' turn came next. U-Boats had a couple of German Stuka-bombers to supply more **Very Lights** and joined the eerie dance.

The Captain rushed down to us: *"Boys! get down into your cabins. We are being attacked. You may be hit by shrapnel."* I said, *"Sir, we would prefer to wear our life-jackets and be ready to jump into the sea rather than been*

---

[33] **Axis powers**: *Britain & France were called **Allies**; Germany & Italy, **Axis***

[34] **Very Lights**: *Military Flares which light up for about 10 seconds to enable aiming at targets. (Pronounced: **VEERY**).*

drowned like rats in our cabins." Captain: "Aren't you afraid?" Self: "No Sir. Only our bodies will die and they will do so sometime or other." Captain: "I can't understand you. Do what you like."

My reply recalled relevant verses of the Bhagawad Gita's in the IInd Canto in which it is stated that the Soul is always intact and immortal; nothing can destroy it.

Of 47 ships, 43 had been blown up; only 4 survived. May be the U-Boats had run out of torpedoes. The 4 Captains awaited dawn, in case there were survivors from the defunct ships. There were none. Some corpses were picked up, stitched into bags, and thrown into the ocean after prayers.

Vignette 16. Voyage-III B

Freetown—Durban—Colombo/Chennai

August to November '42

We reached Freetown top speed. The City of Hong Kong (**C of HK**) was moored alongside the dock. Next to us was the magnificent British Warship, the HMS REPULSE, second Flagship of the British fleet. I had seen her in Plymouth along with my schoolmates. I shouted across and told them about my previous visit. They were delighted and shouted greetings back. It had taken us over 60 days from Glasgow to reach Freetown. HMS REPULSE had made it in 7 days. It was being camouflaged for the tropics.

It was decided that we should sail away unaccompanied, skirting the southernmost tip of Africa, Cape of Good Hope. So we did, it took us 18 days. We had not been allowed to go ashore at Freetown; only water was replenished and urgent needs of the kitchen. Goodbye to free wine! We reached Durban, capital of Natal and most important Southeast African port. Mahatmaji, Mohandas Karamchand Gandhi had spent several years there and made his name for facing up to Apartheid, (discrimination of Blacks and Coloureds by the Whites).

When nearing Durban, we were supposed to be out of the War Zone. Contact with Durban was possible wirelessly. Thomas Cook's Tourist Company had contacted us suggesting tours within Durban and near about. It included an African Reservation. I suppose, because I was the favourite of the elderly ladies, I was requested to arrange for the needful, including making bookings and payments. All of us Indians, and twice as many other passengers were booked to tour Durban. Money was collected by me at £5 each. C of HK was to stay in Durban for 3 days to make it ship-shape after its over 2-month voyage through the Mother of all Storms. This meant we had to forget our sea-legs. The 3 days didn't include the nights to be spent in our cabins. We left daily after breakfast and reappeared for dinner if we wished to, or a little later if we dined out.

It was fairly short shore-leave, our sea-legs were quite ready for the further voyage to Colombo.

When the ship docked at Durban harbour, Thomas Cook's representative made a beeline for me apropos our trip to "Native Africa" and other tours. Beholding my brown face, his lower jaw dropped. He said "You're not English? Your name sounded English, (I had given it as V.S.Charry) when I had confirmed the bookings. *Are you Eurasian at least? All of you can't go together. In South Africa; there is **Apartheid**. You Indians can't travel with Whites. And we no other bus to spare we can only take Whites.*" I told him that I thanked God I was not Eurasian, or Anglo-Indian, but a pure blooded Indian Hindu and proud of it. But we had no colour prejudice. He apologized and said that his hands were tied. We Indians accompanied our non-Indian shipmates to see them off in the bus in front of Cooks' Office. As we were bidding goodbye, a beautiful limousine drew up. An elderly Indian stepped out. He greeted us knowing that we were all Indians too and introduced himself as Kajee. We found out later that he was one of the most well-off Indians of South Africa, and a Muslim. We told him about our plight. *"You're all my guests. Please allow me to be your host throughout your stay here. Do you need Hotel accommodation?* " We were most grateful and told him that we would return to our cabins every evening, and have our dinner aboard. He said, we should, as his guests, also accept dinner. We gladly agreed. He asked whether we were really interested in going to the African Reservation. We said we were. Not to trouble him, we would go by bus. "By no means," said he, "you see I have sent for two more limousines. Oh! They have come! Drop me on the way at my office and the drivers will overtake the bus for the Whites. I advise you not to talk to them when you meet them in the Reservation. There will be trouble if you do." *"Goodbye. Enjoy yourselves."*

The Reservation was, to us, unpleasant. The Africans did not look happy but they smiled to us which they didn't to our White shipmates who were near us. Although they had been extremely friendly aboard, the whites seemed not to see us. We didn't mind one bit and ignored them. Apartheid fever had already infected them; neither were we anxious doctors to cure them. It was surprising how readily Xenophobia is transmitted; those white shipmates, most of them, women had been, shockingly familiar with Indian co-passengers on the decks after dinner before Durban even though most of them were mothers. After Durban, they looked askance at us. We reciprocated.

Next morning, after breakfast, leaving **C of HK**, what should we see but HMS Repulse! We 19 Indians went to the General Post Office to telegraph our near and dear in India and, in my case Malaya, about our welfare. There were two queues at the telegraph counter; one with 3 ladies and the other with a completely idle counter clerk. Naturally some, including me, joined the shorter queue. A tall burly uniformed commissaire approached me, the first Indian in the queue behind the ladies. Without speaking, he tapped me on the shoulder. He out pointed with his thumb to me and the others to join the longer queue. I asked, Why? he pointed to a notice behind the clerk at the window and said *"Can't you read.?"* The notice read, **Voor für Blanken."** It was in the Cape Dutch, language of the Boers. I told my companions that it meant: *"Only for Whites."* I shrugged my shoulders. I had already been victim of Apartheid and got used to it. We all shifted to the long line. Then came a man who looked Chinese. We later found that he was not Chinese but Japanese. The commissaire repeated his gesture and wanted to shoo him too to the long line for "natives."The short "Chinese" took no notice. The guard pushed him roughly by the shoulder. The little gentleman immediately delivered a karate blow on the fellows right shoulder, and in one blow the giant was stretched on the floor face downwards; holding his shoulder as he got up with difficulty. The short gentleman softly but quite audibly told him that he, the piglet, had laid his hand roughly on a subject of the **Mikado** (Emperor of Japan) and he produced his card. The guard went painfully to his post at the door nursing his hurt. The Japanese politely bowed to us. *"Gentlemen, I apologise for this scene. White pigs do not understand any civilized language. They only understand force. Your great Gandhi is too weak for them. They need a good lesson. Japan will give it."* He sent his telegram, bowed to us, went out with the guard still nursing his right shoulder. The Japanese cleared his throat and spat on the road, near the guards foot and calmly strode away. We sent our telegrams. I felt envious of the Little Man. We had not seen the last of him. Next morning, our last in Durban, the Little Man reappeared; he approached **C of HK,** waving to us. When we all came down, he asked us to stand in a line facing him. He had the HMS Repulse in front of him and behind us. He took a photograph of us and said goodbye. I anticipate the future and conclude that it was no coincidence that the background of his photograph of us was **HMS Repulse.** It, along with the brand new, and supposedly unsinkable, **HMS Prince of Wales,** was sunk by the Japanese before the end of the year by their two *Kamikaze* fighters who sacrificed their lives by flying into the funnels of the two greatest Warships of Britain's fleet. Its redoubtable Naval base in Singapore was likewise conquered soon after.

On our last day in Durban, we had seen all reminders of Gandhiji in South Africa; the South African Indian's achievements in education and other fields; and, had enjoyed *Ek Naya Sansār,* my first Indian film. We were deeply beholden to Mr. Kajee and thanked him most gratefully and left. Years later, Miss Kajee was my daughter Ramā Dévi's classmate in a boarding school in England. She along with Ramā spent holidays with us in Frankfurt.

C of HK took us in a week to our last port, Colombo in Ceylon, now Sri Lanka. Travel on the sea was still quite not over. After a days of sightseeing in Colombo and its environment, most of us the Indians were to leave the ship and go by train to Talaimanár, then by Indian ferryboat across Palk Strait, along Adam's Bridge to Dhanushkodi in Tamil Nadu near Rāmeshwaram. Adam's Bridge is said to be the reef constructed by the monkey horde who were the chief troops of Sri Rama when he attacked Ravana's Lanka. The horde hopped over the reefs to attack Lanka.

My ticket was valid from Glasgow to Kolkata (then Calcutta). One of my Indian shipmates, Ramaswamy, who had been a trainee sent by the British India Cannon Factory in Ishapur, Bengal, had his ticket only up to Colombo. Upon reaching Colombo, **C of HK's** Captain received an official telegram instructing him that Ramaswamy should **not** disembark at Colombo, but proceed directly to Calcutta, paying for the extra journey which would be reimbursed to him eventually. Poor Ramaswamy hadn't enough money. The Captain agreed that he could swap his ticket for mine, I should get off in Colombo and he should proceed to Calcutta on my ticket. I had already got off the ship to sight see Colombo. The ships' agent told me about the deal. As I had no commitment in Calcutta and actually preferred to go directly to Madras, it was alright for me to swap. Ramaswamy also sent a message with his request and gave me his elder brother's address in Chennai where I could stay for some time. All my luggage was safely sent to me, and his taken back to the ship. This change of plans was another crucial happening that determined my life. I had not anticipated the Japanese conquest of all British territory in S.E. Asia and my being cut off from my home in Malaya. I had booked for Calcutta to board a ship thence for Singapore. By the end of October, having reached Chennai, I had no alternative but to fend for myself.

My Indian shipmates on **C of HK** visited the temple of Sri Rama in Rameshwaram. On a day's halt in the Railway retiring room in Madurai, we visited Madurai Meenakshi Temple and the Naik's palace. The architecture of the temple affected me deeply, more even that did later the Taj Mahal. The Taj Mahal had no depth and was more or less like a black and white photograph, whereas the Temple was multi-dimensional and the individual carvings, studies in stone as does Leonarda Da Vinci's Mona Lisa. Next day we spent a night in the retiring room of Madras, Egmore station. The following morning, I saw all my shipmates off to Delhi by the Grand Trunk Express. I was all alone in the world.

I hired a Jatka, a one-horse shay with a covered board to sit on. My belongings left one foot of the board for me to sit upon in the rear. I sought Ramaswamy's brother's home at Number 1, Lakshmipuram, Royapettah, Madras. It was raining cats and dogs. The No. 1 was not in serial order; it was the first house built somewhere on that road. It was already 11.am. Evidently it was a middle-middle class area. All the men-folk had left for their daily occupations. I was unfortunately still little too light a shade of brown. I almost look like a *chattekáran,* (shirt-wearer, meaning Eurasian and, therefore, a *mlechhá,* foreigner). When I rapped or knocked on each door, the housewife opened the door a couple of inches, ready to bang it on my face after dismissing me. After that they looked at me through the window to see what I was up toxin my still half-forgotten Tamil, I had told her my name, address and reason, informing her that Mr. Ramaswamy must have sent advance information. *"This is not the house"* was the invariable response. The Jatkawala was restive and the poor pony obviously on its last legs. I had my woolen overcoat on. I was wet from outside and perspiring inside What to do? There was one house, hopefully No.1, at the corner of the side street and the main. It was the last hope before I returned to the Egmore retiring room to ponder and pray to God for help. At this last house I started my litany: *"My name is Charry; I am a friend of Ramaswamy. His brother's address is No. 1 Royapettah. Ramaswamy told me that he would telegraph my name and my date of coming for a couple of days of shelter."* This time, it was no lady who had opened the door; a boy, about 18 gazed at me. His eyes opened wide. He asked, *"Are you lawyer Charry's son? "Yes," Are you from Malaya, from Johore Bahru?""Yes, of course." "Don't you recognize me? I am Bhaskar, brother of your best friend Harihar and son of your teacher Mr. Annadorai Iyer."* A beautiful, elderly lady came from behind Bhaskar. *"My dear son, what brings you back to me?"* I was ready to burst into tears. I had come to the only house in the world which was dearer to me even than my home in Malaya. I had been Meenakshiamma's pet for 3 years, 1930-'33, and used to be joined by Harihar on our way to school. They were of my own *Gothra,* and so I was a family member of which, therefore, the daughters were my sisters. The Infinite had anticipated my prayers. The Jatkawala was delighted by the extra tip that my foster mother insisted on paying in addition to the fare. A minute later, Harihar himself returned cycling. He said that he had caught sight of me on his way out. Seeing only my profile, he had thought that there was something familiar about it.

Altogether I was there for over a month, completely at home. Much happened that will be subject of another Vignette.

CAREER EVENTS AND VOCATION

Vignette 17. Vocation

Brāhmanic Principles assume that in the worldly theatre the supreme objective is solely to act in such a manner that one bids adieu to the **Māya** (illusion) of Life on Earth. Everybody's profession is not necessarily one's vocation. A Brāhmana must become a teacher, always of himself, and as a profession, of children, youths and scholars. He has to prepare himself well to teach those who wish to be taught including himself, his perpetual pupil. If successful, he becomes able in this life or the next, to graduate to *Parabrāhmanism, (eternal bliss)*.

To achieve this objective, the easiest profession for him is teaching children, the more the merrier. He is an actor on his stage; the part he plays is that of Teacher or Tutor. He must be word-perfect; need no prompter; must make others' children his own, eventually considering them as himself. Sincere teaching becomes indissoluble like marriage of two or more intellects. I am reminded or Rigoletto singing his famous and amusing āria: *La Donna ẽ mobilẽ (*The lady is fickle). His voice was tickling laughter but deep in his heart he was grieving deeply at the same time. Were he a Brāhamana, he would also concentrate on the vanity of human affairs, and on bliss eternal.

The teacher and the taught both become noble in character, and accomplished in their careers. Professional achievement of every student is the teachers' guerdon or recompense. When his pupils reach their apices, he rejoices even more satisfied than when he reached his own apex.

In my eleventh year, we, of Std. VII, were told to write an essay on what career each of us would choose. My first line was; "*I have no choice; I am born to be teacher;* my name itself, *Āchārya* means **Teacher**. I did not know then that Āchārya meant, not merely an elementary school, but also one who unravelled to students, the mysteries of Vedic metaphysics and the objective of Life.

I returned to India from Oxford in November 1941 after a 100–day voyage from Glasgow to Colombo and thence to my homeland. World War II had, unlike the First, had embroiled more than half the world, twice as extensive as the previous. With Japan joining the **Axis** powers, hostile to the **Allies,** my parents were thereby cut off from me. They were house prisoners of the Japanese in Johore-Bāhru immediately north of Singapore. I, in Madrās with only £5 left, desperately needed to earn a living. I supposed, I could teach English; I had a fairly good degree in English language and Literature from Oxford; I was taught by distinguished (and by me revered) scholars, C.S. Lewis, Tolkien and Wrenn. I had directed and acted in plays, both English and Indian; initiated the practice of stressing Indian culture in the Oxford Majlis' (Indian Students Association) of which I had been President in my final term. I had spoken in the Oxford Union. As most Oxonians, I was a sportsman; I indulged in hockey, squash, badminton, rowing, (I had coxed the Magdalen Eight). I qualified for hockey only because I was an Indian with no expertise in the game, and so, thankfully, was politely dropped. Fortunately, I also spoke Hindustani and knew **Devanagāri** alphabet. This has enabled me to teach the pronunciation of English words, usually met with in the bizarrely absurd English use of the totally inadequate and unscientific Roman alphabet as used in English.

I landed the job in response to my application in reply to an advertisement in the Statesman sent to me from Kolkata by a friend, Krishnaswamy. Fortunately for me he was a WOG: he read the Statesman instead of Amrita Bazaar Patrika which was for ordinary Indians like me. He sent me a cutting, advertising for an English Teacher in Doon School, Dehra Dun. I later found out that the Viceroy of India who was the Supremo of Doon. The reply from Doon was an appointment letter enclosing a most welcome cheque for Rs.200. I thanked the Almighty: I was *paisa*-less, and would have had, most shamefully, to beg my newly found maternal grandfather to lend me the dough to reach Dehra Dun.

My reception by Doon's Head Master, Mr. Foot, was most cordial. Subsequent drolleries were many.

> *"Before I can tell my life what I want to do with it,*
> *I must listen to my life telling me who I am."*
> *Parker J. Palmer*

Vignette 18. Doon School

Living in the Doon School was idyllic. Except when asleep, all work was play. My suite[35] was one of three rooms; sitter, sleeper, bather-cum-rear[36] on the first floor of the Jaipur House.[37] I was a bachelor assistant master. The first floor was also of a dormitory. It had a narrow corridor-verandah. As Doon[38] was in the foothills of the Himalaya, the weather was pleasantly warm in summer and un-harshly cold in winter. The height of heat and depth of cold happened during vacations. Occasionally, there would have been snowfall, but I would miss it. However, on the northern horizon, 2000 feet higher than Dehra Dun, Mussoorie was visible. Before we left for holidays, we would see Mussoorie wearing a snow-cap; in the nights its lights were like a galaxy in heaven.

School campus covered a 100 acres. Earlier it had been the Forest Research Institute. Hence, I was blessed with a repeat of my English school's demi-paradise and my college in Oxford. The tress had grown to

---

[35] suite: (pronounced "sweet"), Sets of rooms in 5-Star Hotels (very expensive (!))

[36] Rear: Oxonian for "Toilet"

[37] Jaipur House: in my time, there were four main Houses, Hyderabad, Jaipur, Kashmir and Tata.Names indicating their Donors: 2 Maharajas, 1 Nizam and Tata Company. There was also a 3rd known as Clough House which was for youngest fresher's. It was on the main road facing the Campus, named Mr. Clough.

[38] Doon: Dehra Dun is now capital of Uttarakhand, formerly part of Uttar Pradesh, earlier known as U.P. (United Provinces of Agra & Oudh). I discovered, being etymologically curious, what the connection was between DUN and Doon: DEHRA DUN means "Tent Valley"; Doon was the English spelling of DUN. "DUN" in English means "bailiff." Isn't it a clever way of distinguishing them?

their full heights. Apart from spacious evergreen lawns (for games) there was a whole catalogue of verdure.

As celibate assistant master, I had the not-too-pleasant duty of inspecting the dormitories of the first floor of Jaipur House. It was meant to discourage brutish misdemeanour. But it also meant forgoing my beauty-sleep and also interrupting my sleep again: first Inspection at 10 to 10:20pm; second round, alarm awakened, 2 to 2:20am. I had to be up an hour before dawn. It was some alleviation, having worked from 7am to 1pm, to have a siesta of about an hour and a half before afternoon school and games which went on till sunset. Altogether, life was healthy and pleasurable for me till I was 24; and then, when I got me a wife, it was even healthier and blissful. I am happy that it continues to be so at 93.

When I reached Dehra Dun, I was met by a Doon maintenance staff member. He escorted me on a tonga, a delightfully memorable little journey: my Hindi passed muster and so had already made a charming admirer and friend. After breakfast, I was summoned by the Headmaster and introduced to Milady Mrs. Foot who invited me to breakfast. I politely declined as I had had my fill. Then, the Head gazed at me, up and down, and smiled; I had passed muster. "I have a surprise for you" said he. "According to our rules, laid down by his Excellency the Viceroy, perhaps absent-mindedly,the Block-Head of our School Faculties has to be the best qualified in the subject. I see that you are the one best qualified in the English faculty. Therefore, you have to convene every Saturday forenoon, a hebdominal[39] meeting of all our English Teachers in the Teachers' Common Room. You have to chair it. I wish you luck."

> *Somewhat amused, I asked, "Block-head? What do you mean."*
> *He said somewhat sharply, "The Head of the Block"*
> *Coolly but gently, I retorted, "Would you look it up in a dictionary?"*
> *Peevishly, he did so. He burst out laughing. "Which idiot suggested that term. I hope it wasn't me!" "What should it be?"*
> *"Faculty Head would be the proper term."*
> *"Thank you very much indeed. You will be head of the English Faculty."*

---

[39]   Hebdominal : Weekly (ā la Ox-Cam).

I had no clue as what could happen at my first Hebdominal. There was no Minute Book. I was given a list of duties which would take up 16 hours on weekdays, apart from the 2 aforesaid excursions at night. There was much action on sports fields and extracurricular activities. They included my weekly tutorials of 15 boys of Jaipur House. This last was well suited to my Brāhmanic temperament: I was to become a Guru of 15 Sishyās[40]

The first English Faculty meeting was astonishing to me; my 5 fellow English teachers were all Englishmen. I felt, I was a brownie[41] not even a Scout cub. I was not yet 22. Youngest of the 5 was 42; the next 3 were nearing 50, and the remaining gentleman 55. They were all House Masters and at best benevolent tyrants (and rarely despots) over 50 children in each House.

Our first hebdominal was at 11am around an oval table. There were two gentlemen on either long side and one at the bottom; at the other end a high chair for the Chairman. Incidentally, my pay was Rs.200 pm with perks of food and my suite; their emoluments started from Rs.2500 with 3 double-bedroom bungalows each, even though only one was married, Mr. Clough of Clough House.

All five were seated. To my amazement, they stood up, upon my entry. In one voice they said "Welcome, Sir" and sat down only after "Sir" sat. None of them had come from Oxford, Cambridge or even London, nor had they taken English as their degree subject. They seemed to be happy about my having been empowered to render them any needed assistance. My totally unconscious and unintended pronunciation of the first line of Chaucer's Prologue to the Canterbury Tales delighted them. My début as Faculty primus dominus was satisfactory. I am truly grateful to my Pentagon for 3 Years and 3 Months of unsurpassable camaraderie.

---

[40]   *Guru/Sishyas: Metaphysical Teacher and acolytes*
[41]   *Brownie: a little very young Girl-Guide. I used to be called "Brownie" by small boys in England because of my colour.*

Vignette 19. Novice Teacher-I

Even now, after half-a-century, I am surprised that I had dared to become a teacher of English, and felt at home in my vocation, in 'as to the manner born.' I had insufficient paper qualifications; no Teachers' Training, B.Ed., and no previous experience as is insisted upon in India today, I do not know why. All I had was my black Oxford B.A. graduate gown. I coped with all my tasks. About **Language Teaching**, would it not be better to recruit teachers without burdening them with irrelevances such as they actually to go to acquire their B.Eds.? I have encountered many such teachers who have not benefitted by their B.Eds. I am positive that a trainee should already be a regular teacher, at least half-time, in a school. He/She should be assisted weekly during two periods by the English Faculty Head in the regular School. I do think that genes matter. In India, there are already families who had been teachers for generations.

Oral teaching is more effective than only book reading by teacher and pupils. Most teachers simply read out text books; they do not express themselves. Next, I have found that quickest success is through using poetry and drama, and definitely not, in English, prose. Poetry should be chosen carefully: they should be "actable." Louis Carrol's **Walrus and Carpenter** is a fine poem for the purpose. Another is Browning's **Pied Piper**; a third is selected stanzas of Coleridges's **Ancient Mariner**. These can be made into ***Tableaux Récitatifs***[42]. We have tried them out; found them most entertaining, memorable and excellent sources for acquiring vocabulary, spelling, grammar and "wise saws and modern instances." Children of 11—12 should have memorized, at least six such gems each year from Std. II to V. They will have something to treasure lifelong.

When problematic English words cropped up, I took care not to spell them in the inadequate Roman alphabet, further polluted in its English

---

[42] ***Tableaux Récitatifs*** : *Poems which are acted with a narrator to introduce and provide links between stanzas, and, if need be, an Epilogue*

rendering. I pronounced the word slowly in the best accent I could summon. Then they were written on the blackboard in the Devanagari script of Sanskrit. Finally, when English spelling was put on the board the children would have their laugh. We had fun with words like ***through, though, bough,* brough**t. Once English begins to be spoken fluently—as they are with English children—grammar just happens. Let us remember there was no grammar book for the writer (unknown) of Beowulf, Chaucer, Shakespeare, Milton, Dryden, Pope and even Dr. Johnson himself in the mid-18th century. In fact, English lexicography began to be compiled properly, for the first time by Dr. Johnson. In a way, the greatness of Shakespeare in particular lay because he was not inhibited by grammar books or dictionaries; he was free to write as he willed and became the greatest English writer ever. Classical languages, such as Sanskrit, need grammar only because they are not spoken commonly, and have relatively regular declensions of nouns and pronouns, conjugations of verbs and regular endings of degrees in adjectives and adverbs.

In so far as English teaching was concerned, feedback from parents of children in Ācārya Vidya Kula is encouraging, although they don't have a clue on how the results were achieved.

I have happy recollection of directing and teaching dramas. Successes in Doon School and Ācārya Vidya Kula were: **Flecker's Hassan, Poetasters of Ispahan, Little Man, Macbeth, St. Joan, Aeschylus' Persians** and portions of Gilbert's Operas particularly **Mikado, Gondoliers, Iolanthe and Yeomen of the Guard**, and several *Tableaux Récitatifs.* I hope there are some Doon pupils who recall the thrills they experienced. One of them, Lovraj Kumar, went as a Rhode's Scholar not only to Oxford but also to my *Alma Matter*, Magdalen. Alas! he is no more.

The teacher who is indeed wise does not bid you
to enter the house of his wisdom
but rather leads you to the threshold of your mind.
Khalil Gibran

Vignette 20. Novice Teacher-II

My last 6 months in Doon were enjoyed even more than the previous 2 ½: I was also honey-mooning. I reached the advanced age of 24; my bride even more advanced 'common sensibly' at 14 ½. Being married, we were allotted a 2 bedroom cottage, one for guests. We were surrounded by 50 trees. Forty of them yielded bumper crops of *lichis*. The trees were contracted out by the school for a good fee. Falling in love with us, the contractor gifted generous portions of the fruit. The Malayan *rambutan* looks like, but is not a patch on the Indian *lichi*.

Āndāl was my bride. For short, I called her "Dāl"; she became a favourite on the campus; she cooked dinner only twice a week. Breakfast and lunch were free and compulsory for both of us throughout Term. In Jaipur House dining hall, she was soon at home. She sat at the opposite end of the table headed by me. How the boys hastened to sit right and left of her! How much more noise they made than those next to me! She was still tom-boyish enough to be like an elder sister; she had no brothers of her own.

Leaving Doon on 30th April, 1945 was bitter-sweet. Bitter because the official *de jure*, Head of Doon was the Viceroy of India. Doon was perhaps meant to fabricate brown Sahibs. To placate minorities, hopefully allies of the Raj, the Viceroy directed Mr. Foot, immediately to recruit Muslim and Christian teachers to maintain "communal harmony." Naturally, Foot had to obey the *de jure* Head; result: Disharmony! Our new colleagues were virtual non-entities; they could hardly make themselves understood. From the start, they cold-shouldered the Hindus; the English Teachers cold-shouldered them. I, non-communalist but ardent nationalist, wished to resign. My morale was boosted by a similar decision by friend Ameer Ali who told me he would follow suit when found another job. His uncle was the noted ornithologist, Salim-Ali, a Shia Muslim. Ameer found a good post with the International Labour Organization (ILO) in Geneva. Saying goodbye to my dear Classes and my dearer *shishyāh* of 15 in Jaipur House overcame me. For days, not even my Andāl could console me. Time healed.

Mr. Clough, one of my Faculty colleagues, had left soon after the incursion of the "minorities." He landed a fine job in the Publications Division of the Information Department of the British Indian Government. I had invited him for my wedding in Bangalore. He regretted his inability to attend and invited me to call on him in Delhi *en route* to Dehra Dun. I did. Apart from a generous wedding-gift, he offered me a senior job in the Publications Division just below his own. I would be the 3rd most senior in the Division. He gave me 3-months to think it over. I did. Before I resigned in Doon I wrote to him, and he confirmed my appointment. I became Head of Eastern Division, preparing publicity material for East and South Asia: China, Indonesia; and, westwards, all Arab countries. The serenity of Dehra Dun and perks of free breakfast and lunch during School Terms would be missing. But, in Delhi, the remuneration of Rs.700 per month and government quarters at 5% of salary, more than made up for the loss of perks. Distance to my office room from my Government suite was even less than that from my Doon bungalow to the class rooms. ***Purana Daphtar*** (Old Secretariat), the Office, was just across Alipur Road, barely a five-minute walk. The Old Secretariat with its veranda right around outside the building was incomparably more comfortable than the Secretariat in New Delhi, built by Lutyens. His verandas went round the *inside of the building.*

My suite was only as big as my bachelor accommodation in Doon. Being wartime, it was well below my entitlement. Hence its rent was 5% instead of the normal 10%. We were happy in it. By good fortune, my wife's aunt and husband's flat was a mere 5-minute cycling away. We had arrived in Delhi station on 1st May, 1944. We were met by an office peon and blistering heat. We left in a tonga[43] for our suite. Aunt Sharada, (nicknamed Auntie Awful—most undeservedly—had sent her servant, inviting us for lunch and dinner for a few days, before we settled down.

---

[43] **tonga**: a one-horse shay meant for 4 passengers with luggage tied up on top. (Thank heaven; we possessed just the luggage for the front seat and top; the peon preceded us on cycle.)

Our extended Indian family was truly generous throughout the life time of that affectionate couple whose only children we became.

> *The important thing is not so much that every child should be taught,*
> *as that every child should be given the wish to learn.*
>
> *John Lubbock*

Vignette 21. Why Not Indian Civil Service-I (ICS)?

Answer: a longish Saga, I fear, almost like the **Nibelungenlied**[44]; and as "Incredible" which India is now supposed to be. Briefly, however, the answer is: " I am perverse."

My father was a WOG. My grandfather was a conformist and conformed to all the rules and regulations of Her/His Britannic Majesty and retired, duly entitled as the topmost native in His/Her Military Audits and Accounts Service. My father said that he would never be a servant but always a master. He had an M.A. besides he was a Barrister of the Lincoln's Inn where the best Wines were served. Paradoxically, when in Malaya whither he wended to seek his fortune, he became a "Retainer" of the British Straits Settlements and at the same time "Retainer" of His Highness the Sultan of Johore. This should have absolved him from having to earn petty cash as a Lawyer. It didn't. He practiced to great effect and delighted English Judges who, metaphorically, wore him like their native pearl tie-pin. Consequence: he won his cases and petty cash which was not so petty. He also had all the appurtenances of a thorough WOG: tobacco, pipe and binoculars for the Singapore races. Like a gentleman, he unerringly put his shirt on the favourite horse when it lost. This being the case, he wouldn't have been too unhappy if I had been chosen for the Indian Civil Service. Grandpa, of course, would have said "Whoopee!"My mother would have echoed him on a higher note. But then, I was and still am Perverse.

I am most grateful to my father for most important things: for teaching me by example what not to do, and also even more, for teaching

---

[44] ***Nibelungenlied:*** *A series of four long Operas by Wagner including Siegfreid and Valkyrie. It is also known as the Ring of the Nibelungs, dwarves who kept a golden ring in the Rhine river.*

me what to do. He taught me how to speak, to be self-dependent at need; to be a mechanic, do the humblest work proudly and as well I could; to out-English him in English; to beat him in chess; to familiarize myself with the Bhagawad Geeta and, unlike him not to ignore its teaching and postpone it for the next life.

It was towards the end of my 8th and 2nd last term, in Oxford. Apparently, I was tagged by the Professor of Sanskrit of Oxford University even as were, a few other selected abnormalities among the Indian undergrads. Obviously his report must have been favourable. As a member of Oxford Majlis, I had achieved other things besides talking politics and complaining about such things as the English weather and Indian slavery. For the first time in Oxford, I had staged several Indian Plays such as *Mrichhakatika* of Bāna, Tagore's *Post Office* and *Sacrifice*. I had organized competitions like Quizzes on India and Indian English. I was a Wet Bob as the Cox of the Magdalen First Eight boat; played a fairly good game of squash (to keep down my weight as cox); I was an ardent cyclist and had pedalled a 1000 miles a year for 2 years. (I did a further 1000 miles in my last year). I was a member of all the Political Clubs including the Conservative, flaunting my complete loyalty to His Highness the Maharaja of Mysore and approving Duleepsinghji and Ranjeethsinghji, the Indian cricketing noblemen. In Magdalen, my moral tutor, the Reverend Adam Fox must have told them about the lovely evenings we had together, pleasantly discussing our adherences to our respective ethics and morals.

To top it all, I had accidently met the Head of the India Office, Mr. Stafford Cripps, in the Vega Restaurant in Leicester Square, London. He had been lunching with George Bernard Shaw (GBS). When I wished to enter Vega, the commissionaire at the door told me loudly that I had please to wait as there was no free seat yet. From the rear, a shrill male voice shouted *"You're wrong. There are two seats available here at our table. Send him in."* I went in. I recognized both gentleman from their pictures in newspapers. Everybody knew Shaw. The Simon Commission had returned from India and famously failed. There had been hot discussion about Irish and Indian Freedom.

GBS: *"Excellent! You look like an Indian. Are you?"*

VSC: *"Yes Sir"*

GBS: *"How lucky we are Cripps. (to me) What you know about Ireland?"*

VSC: *"I know the Deserted Village and why it was deserted and also know about the Massacre on some Bloody Day. I forget whether it was a Saturday or Sunday. It was something like the Massacre of Jallianawala Bagh in Amritsar, Punjab."*

Cripps(C): *"I agree. Both were shameful. Tell me, young man, what's your name? and what you study, if you do study."*

VSC: *"Yes Sir, my name is Charry. I am from Magdalen, Oxford. I study English Language and Literature with Mr. C.S. Lewis."*

Both GBS and C: *"Excellent arbiter."*

GBS: *"Do you like the British?"*

VSC: *"Yes, I like the English very much at home. Abroad, they are stupid and snooty."*

C: *"Why do you call them stupid?"*

VSC: *"They think too much of themselves and don't know how to be civil. Besides, no country can afford to send really educated people abroad. There are too few of them for their own country. Except for the Irish, because, they have been fleeced."*

GBS: *"Why do you think that the Irish were fleeced?"*

VSC: *"Again, because the English and even the Scots in Ireland felt that they were superior people, and some Irish fawned upon them. It required great leaders like **Éamon de Valera** to inspire them, another reason seems to me that too many Irish allow themselves to be recruited into the British Armed Forces and become expendable cannon fodder."*

C: *"What does your father do?"*

VSC: *"He is a Barrister in the Straits Settlements.*

C: *"Would you like India to become Independent?"*

VSC: *"We are no different from the British. We would like to be like them in so far as governance is concerned. I don't think that an Englishman would be happy in India if he were truly educated. Those who like India, I find, are only those who like others to do menial jobs. The poor in India have no choice but to do them. I feel that imperialism is most deleterious to the imperialists themselves. It spoils their character more than wealth does."*

After conversation with GBS, the Lunch was over. Later, when I got a call from India Office, to fill an application form for the ICS, I had a hunch that the lunch was responsible for it.

VIGNETTE 22. WHY NOT INDIAN CIVIL SERVICE-II

At the end of Hilary Term in April, the Oxford Majlis decided to announce the next Terms' Officers. I was the obvious candidate because, I was already Secretary. The convention was for the Secretary to be become automatically the next President. Before that happened, there was a debate in the Oxford Union concerning India. The Motion was: In the opinion of this House *"India should be given Independence immediately."* I opted to speak against the Motion. The Majlis members were aghast. They said that I would never be elected as President of Majlis. The debate was to take place within a couple of days and it was too late to change. In that case, I was told, that I could not be President of Majlis.

We must remember that War was on. Blackouts occurred from time to time when German bombers were flying over England on their grim tasks. Sometimes the lights went out even within houses. The Union debating hall was full, with curtains drawn to prevent any light being spotted from the sky. The Proposer had duly spoken. I led the Opposition. As always, my speech was impromptu. The gist was: Nothing given is ever prized. A country which got its freedom on a silver platter would lose it soon. India had to continue to fight for it peacefully and Britain go out gracefully and unconditionally. Meanwhile, Indian soldiers should not be commanded by non-Indians. According to our thinking, everybody and every country got what they deserved; that was the theory of *Karma* which was the basis of Indian Metaphysics. As I said this, the lights went out for a few minutes. German bombers were over Oxford on their flight towards Birmingham and Coventry. All were told to sit in their places. I had to stand because there was no seat behind me. When the lights came on, I continued saying that all suffering was due to bad *Karma*. Evil had to be resisted before it could be overcome by good *Karma*. Indian Independence did not depend in the final analysis on any one else except the Indian people themselves. When the debate ended, the Proposer lost. I had proved that we were not to take gifts but deserve what we wanted. I became President of Majlis.

Towards the end of June, I was called for an interview in India House, London. The head of the India House then an Indian, a notable Anglophile. He presided, and didn't say a word. All others were Englishmen from India Office. Our conversation was surprisingly casual. I was asked if I was interested in the Indian Civil Service. I replied that my first love was teaching. Then I was told that in the Oxford Union, a few weeks earlier I had given the impression that I didn't care for British rule in India. Was that my real opinion or a rhetorical exercise? I said my opinion was that I wanted India to be like any other country. I would like it to be free to choose its own Government. We were not European and I didn't wish to become European even as I would not like Europe to be like India. Our Civilization was different with objectives different from that of Europe. I didn't consider Progress as being material. Real progress was spiritual. That was the object I was brought up to have. Then I was asked if I would retract what I implied about the British India. Truthfully, I said I couldn't do that. I was then told that as a Civil Servant of the British Indian Government, I had to obey orders. Would I do so? I replied that I would not obey orders which went against my principles. With polite words on both sides I took my leave. Later I heard from India Office that I was put on the Waiting List. I heard nothing more thereafter. I left England on 19th August 1941.Later, I found that a junior of mine had been selected.

I was not the least disappointed. My subsequent life has been ideal for me. Had I been in the ICS, I would have missed all that I experienced later. As a member of ICS I certainly would not have been what I am: ***Brāhmanic***.

> *I will undoubtedly have to seek what is happily*
> *known as gainful employment,*
> *which I am glad to say does not describe holding public office.*
> Dean Acheson

Vignette 23. Why Indian Foreign Service (IFS)?

An Interim "Coalition" Government of Congress and Muslim League was installed before Independence. Jawaharlal Nehru headed it nominally. Having charge of External Affairs, he decided to hold an Asian Conference and scheduled it for early May 1946. Asian countries were invited to convene in New Delhi. He wanted a brochure for the Conference. The Publications Division was assigned to produce it. Its Department was under a Muslim League Minister. He was uninterested and left it all to the Director. No better person being willing, I was made responsible for it, in addition to my other chores. I managed to do it. The proof had to be sent to Jawaharalalji. He found time to read it. His noting was telephoned to me: *"Wonderful. Printing okayed. I want to see the writer."* This was embarrassing to me. However, Fate prevented it: he was too busy to keep an appointment for small fry like me in those hectic days. However, Fate effected the appointment!

I met him on the eve (2–5–'46) of the conference venue, ***Lal Qila*** (Red Fort, Delhi). I had been sent along with others to arrange the chairs for the meeting and place the brochures on the seats. While we were toiling, Jawaharlalji entered, unexpected and unannounced. He joined our gang to help! His private secretary pointed me out to him as the Brochure's good (or evil?) genius.

Our conversation was in Hindustani on his part (JN) and in Hindi (VS) on mine.

JN: *Son! Thou art a child!*
VS: *I can't help that. I did what I could.*
JN: *Where didst thou study?*
VS: *In Oxford.*
JN: *Wah! re wah! It's no wonder your work is not bad. What didst thou read?*
VS: *English language and literature*

JN: *Wah! re wah! Not History?*

VS: *One can't read anything without History. Besides, nowadays, there is nothing better to read.*

JN: *Join the Congress. Will you? You'll do well.*

VS:*Sir, I would be out of place.*

JN: *Why?*

VS: *My behaviour would be unsuitable for politicians.*

JN: *But I am Politician, Son.*

VS: *No Sir, you are a Gentleman.*

JN *(patting me)***:** *Ha! Ha! Ha! Then you must join our Foreign Service.*

VS: *I wanted to return to Teaching.*

JN : *Do this for me. It is necessary for the country. Try out diplomacy. You only have to write a thesis.*

VS: *Sir, I shall try.*

JN: *See you later.*

VS: *Namaste*

Original Hindi version in Appendix II

I did try. The thesis was completed by September '47. It was titled, **S.E Asia and Indian diplomatic relations.** I faced a panel of senior ICS officers who, I supposed, had read the thesis. It seemed that it had mystified them. One member of the panel admitted that he knew little about the subject. After several searching questions, answered as quickly as they were put, the Interview was over. I was one of their First choices[45]. I was posted to the Indian Embassy, Brussels, Belgium as Head of Chancery and Political Secretary. I took over on 1ˢᵗ May, 1948.

---

[45] ***First choices:*** *In the '47-48 batch of Foreign Service I became the 73ʳᵈ in the civil list of Foreign Officers. Indian Civil Servants who had opted for IFS and several Indians who had joined Military Service with the British during World War II who had been promised by British Government to be accommodated, were my seniors.*

Vignette 24. Aihole

My first History text book in the English College Johore-Bahru, Johore, Malaya, was understandably, chosen by the British Management even for the Unfederated Johore Malayan State. Its ruler, Sultan Ibrahim was proud of his State being **Un**-federated. Despite his pride, he was unaware of the liberties that the British took to see that the real History of Malay was ignored. My text book gave the impression that there was no History worth studying other than that of the British Empire and possibly of western Europe. I was Indian and proud of our Indic Society, my family title itself being Āchārya. I had been in Patna, Bihar which was conscious of its past. My grandfather was my prime tutor and made me conscious of our heritage.

My text book dealt with the details of how the Empire of the "Nation of Shopkeepers,"—Napoleon's christening of England,—was founded. Unlike its former possession, New England, the northern border of present-day USA, the south Asian possessions were not colonies, whither emigrants from their mother lands became immigrants. Both the Americas, North and South, and Australia are populated not by the natives, but overwhelmingly by natives of Europe. India and South East Asia are still populated almost wholly "natively pearl." It is salutary to note that Angles and Saxons eliminated the real Britons, most of whom were killed, survivors escaping into Wales which became part of "Britain" only after the Norman King Edward-Ist conquered it. It is also curious that England's monarchs were, after 1066 A.C., Norman French, Scot and West German. None of them was Briton or Anglo-Saxon. The present dynasty, basically Hanoverian, changed its name to the House of Windsor. Mountbatten, the last Viceroy of India, was actually Battenberg.

Despite my not having a clue about what has been stated in the last paragraph, I resented English rule in India. It was only because of my knowledge of English that my Welsh History Teacher, Mr. Morgan, put up with my resentment. Perhaps he, himself being Welsh, knowing the above, empathized with me Forgive me. I have almost forgotten to pay a little attention to Aihole (Vide Appendix-V).

My interest in Aihole began with reference to it by Professor V. Subbarayalu of the Tamil University of Tanjavur visiting Mysore on 12th May 1999.He entitled his lecture **"The Aihole Trade Guild in India and Overseas."**I disagreed with his title and felt that it should have been, **Aihole—Deccan Maritime League**. Having considered the matter further, I would now prefer to call it: **"The Deccan East India Company."** It makes sense because, its structure was undoubtedly the foundation of the West European versions including the Merchant Adventurers from England, France, Netherlands and Denmark. All of them wished to by-pass the Turco-Arabs and collar their exorbitant middlemen's profits by skirting the Cape of Good Hope, aptly named Adventurers. They were preceded by the Portuguese who were less interested in commerce and more in saving souls of barbarians like me and my ancestors. Fortunately, the Reformation, Renaissance and the Dutch, who had ceased to be Roman Catholics, whacked them out of Malaysia and Indonesia. Spain too, for a while, took over Portugal. Within India, the Portuguese could only maintain footholds. The Western European Market was the monopoly of the Netherlands, England, France and Denmark.

The Deccan East India Company (DEIC) had its Headquarters in Aihole. It was well situated at the centre of the Deccan. Its tentacles within India certainly stretched right up to the borders of Gujarat in the northwest and **Odissa** (Orissa) in the northeast, their chief ports being Surat and Puri Jagannath respectively. In Odissa it was the Kālingan Empire which was the sponsor. The Aihole phenomenon was not a Guild at all: it did not concern itself with the **manufacture** of any one commodity; nor was its activity confined, like European Guilds, to one locality, city or big town or single commodity. It is analogous, though slightly different in operation, to the **Cinque Ports,** Protestant merchant City-States of north western Europe and the **Hanseatic League**, stretching from Hamburg to Dantzig (Gdansk) in today's Poland. The League's was a cardinal role in Renaissance Europe during the turmoil's that resulted in drastic curbing of Papal hegemony. The Cinque Ports were not independent States, but maintained Commerce during the troubled confrontations in which France, England and the Netherlands under the Hapsburgs.

The DEIC was the most effective and long-lived of such leagues. It was, by all counts a trading Leviathan. This mercantile Banyan had branches or aerial roots, some 100 of them, from Kolhapur in

Maharashtra to East Java (Bali). Obviously, DEIC outstripped the Hanseatic League. Its operations were considerably vaster, extending over 5000 miles from Maratha Territory in India up to Sumatra and Java. Its longevity too was comparatively Methusalan: a whole millennium with its birth in the 8th Century A.D., its apogee possibly in the 10th; and its fade-away in the 18th. The eclectic pragmatism of the DEIC was of the nature of the contemporary Leviathans, the Multi-Nationals who permit no prejudice of race, creed or political credo to impede the flow into their tills. They traded on equal terms with protagonists of non-Hindu faiths, including, in the latter half of its life, Muslims and Buddhists. This clearly indicates the prevalence of commercial over religious or sectarian interests.

Yet, like Venice, and to an extent the Knights of Malta, the DEIC cemented its unity through religion and myth. Their example became prototypical. For, the English Factors' followed their example: they obtained license to construct fortifications, to recruit body guards, to have mutual assistance pacts with local chieftains, to foster Churches. The then Central Governments' simply did not ensure Law and Order. Forts St. George and St. William had DEIC precedents and were, therefore, no pioneering ploys to provide insurance for CIF transactions!

The fading away of the DEIC, significantly coincided with the hegemony over all the South India by the London-based East India Company. Tippu's successes over the Maratha and Keralite Chieftains and his total defeat by the trained Indian sepoys of the English aliens sounded the DEIC death knell.

How much more entertaining is such History than myths about individuals of whom barely anything is known profoundly, such as the ambiguous Tippu Sultan. These cannot be taken seriously being but slanted versions. Instead, facts, guardedly garnered and carefully sifted, such as the actual operations of the DEIC, are far more pertinent and credible.

That men do not learn very much from the lessons of history
is the most important of all the lessons of history.
Aldous Huxley

Vignette 25. Diplomatic Dinner-I

The second half of 1954 is memorable and much cherished by me. Glorious Autumn awaited us in Peking (Beijing). Early in September, I took up my post of First Secretary (Political) and Head of Chancery in our Embassy. China's Sun had risen. Its anthem *Tung*[46] *Fang Hung* translated is "East is Red." Japan's Sun Flag had been lowered; Communism, under Mao Tze-Tung, had cleared out the US supported **Chiang Kai-Shek's** Kuo-Min-Tang (KMT). The KMT, protected by USA, fled, lock stock and barrel, to Taiwan, (formerly Formosa, under the Japanese for 5 decades). They had taken shiploads of cultural treasures; it was one of the best things they did because they escaped rampage by rowdy gangs who swarmed as Mao Tze-Tung's personal capacity dwindled due to old age. The "Gang-of-Four," headed by his last wife, an ex-film star, began to rule the roost. It was my pleasure to have visited, after my retirement, the museum housing the treasure in Taipeh. KMT could also have preserved their ancient Chinese culture of Confucianism. Being under the aegis of the Pentagon, KMT had no time for such trivialities.

October 1954 was important. The USA had launched SEATO[47] with their ex-colony Philippines and its capital Manila as headquarters, Australia as their chief supporter and other underlings including Pakistan. SEATO was supposed to contain the further spread of Communism. Neutralism too was targeted. It had been propounded by true patriots, not congenial to the Pentagon. It was headed by Sukarno of Indonesia, Tito of Yugoslavia, Nasser of Egypt and Nehru of India. The neutral's were to meet during 21st to 24th April, 1955 in Bandung, the beautiful hill-station nearest Jakarta. Prime Minister Nehru's visit to Peking in early October, our Diwali, was timed to do something to strengthen Non-Alignment. Its purpose was to attract China and thereby stabilize

---

[46] **Tung:** *U is pronounced as **oo** in Cool; **A,** as **a** in 'car'*

[47] *SEATO: South East Asian Treaty Organization*

Eastern Asia and make the South and East Asia, with half the population of the World, a truly **Pacific** area. It was in this context that, in a lighter vein, the "Diplomatic Dinner," given by India as protocol demanded, became uniquely memorable.

Our Prime Minister, Jawaharlal Nehru, was received by the Chinese with courtesies equal to that of any Head of State. He was recognized as being completely genuine in his professed neutrality. Tito, too, of Yugoslavia, was as high in China's esteem. Hence, it was obvious that China truly welcomed Nehru's visit. Unfortunately, we received the news of passing away of Rafi Ahmed Kidwai of Uttar Pradesh and dear to Nehru. That was the only cloud that marred the visit.

It is the protocol for visiting VIPs also to return courtesies received by hosting a dinner in return. Naturally, our Embassy had to organize it. Our Ambassador was Sri. Nedyam Raghavan. I had been his Head of Chancery in Brussels, Belgium for a couple of months towards end of 1950. He told me to make the dinner as Indian as possible. Normally, in China, only Chinese food was available in the hotels, however big. Their staff could not provide Indian food. Our Ambassador insisted that the dinner had to have an Indian menu although Chinese food should also be available. I contacted the Chinese Protocol Office and was assured that there would be no objection if making Indian food were the total responsibility of the Indian Embassy.

In all, including security guards, chauffeurs, cleaners, clerks, junior officers, the Military Attaché (MA) and all the other diplomatic officers and their personal Indian servants, we numbered nearly a 100 without the Ambassador and wife and the second most senior Diplomatic Officer, the Counsellor, and wife. About 520 people had to be catered for. There would be 50 tables with 10 diners each and the high table for about 20 VIPs. There would be the topmost members of the Chinese Government headed by Chairman Mao, the Vice-Chairman, the Premier and Foreign Minister Chou En-Lai. There would also be their Holinesses, the Dalai Lama and the Panchen Lama. At the other tables, the Heads of the Diplomatic Missions with their wives and Senior Chinese Government Officers (without wives) would be seated. All our diplomatic staff and one or two members of our Office staff would be at each table. The dinner was to start at 6:45 p.m. and end by 8.Thereafter, all invitees would move to the historic Hall of Tien An Men (Gate of Heaven) where a show would entertain them.

Vignette 26. Diplomatic Dinner-II

Two days before the dinner, wives of all the embassy Indians—except, of course, Ambassador's and Counsellor's—and their servants, the security guards (all of them Sikhs) started cooking, led by their chief, Opar Singh who elected to make *Jilabies*[48].At the request of the Ambassador, who had tasted my wife's cooking, we were to make *onion sāmbār*[49].Fortunately, our Jeeves, Gopalan was game. 520 servings! In which to cook? We bought a man-size bath tub of aluminium with handles at both ends through which a pole could be put to help carrying it to its destination, up the hotel steps, and put into pantry for Indian food adjoining the dining hall, in good time. Other staff were not as bold enough to make food for 500+; they distributed the cooking of the dozen dishes among half a dozen groups.

At About 5:30 p.m., all of us gathered in front of the imposing hotel, Shin Jiao Fan Tien (New palace of heavenly food), if my memory serves me right. It was decorated with festoons and flags. Luckily, it was not far from our Embassy where the food had been kept with pushcarts in readiness. They were trundled to the hotel steps and unloaded by our helping staff. Our silvery bathtub was unloaded last. Two of our sturdy Sikhs put their shoulders to the pole and were approaching the steps, luckily only 6. The hotel supervisors stopped the bathtub to inspect it. The covering was removed. They looked; they smelt it from a safe distance; they shuddered; shook their heads; and asked what it

---

[48] **Jilabies:** *colourful, shining, sticky, honey-sweet, succulent, crunchy, wheaten, in concentric circles one inch in radius ¼ inch thickness, some say the queen of all Indian yum-yum desserts.*

[49] **Sāmbār:** *A Tamil speciality, pungent, salty, made of pulses and condiments with various vegetables the most popular being onions. However, this King of Tamil cooking does not look charming at all. It looks somewhat like what you see when you have not pulled the chain or pressed the button after abdominal relief. I empathise with the Chinese hotel supervisors. (?)*

contained. Our Sikh security guards whispered to them that it was called *Sāmbār*. Inspectors were not enlightened. Opar Singh interpreted to us that the Inspector told him that they would not be responsible if anything happened as a result of that stuff being eaten. After a brief conference among themselves, the supervisors ordered everyone of the Chinese staff to vacate the hotel. They did so and crossed the road and stood at attention, facing the hotel in grim silence.

Our Military Attaché (MA), Brigadier Kochhār, and I have a quick open-air conference of one minute. We decide we would do all the serving ourselves: MA will direct the operations; I head our Platoon. Our wives won't be troubled, they will sit, one each, at some of the general tables; other tables will each have one of our senior staff. All the remaining Indians will be waiters. I and my personal staff of seven will serve the High Table. Opar Singh and two other security guards will hand out the serving dishes at the doors next to the pantries, one on each side, close to the platform of the high table. MA will guard the Indian Food Door; his Lieutenant the Chinese Food Door. All of us, males in our Bandgallās, (the official closed-collar jacket) and white trousers will be not mere waiters, but Servers. MA: *"On your marks! Get Set . . ."* We are all prepared to '*March!*'

The Hall filled up; 500 diners were seated. Some Ambassadors and Chinese Government Officers recognized me and raised their hands. I bowed and they graciously nodded back. The VVIPs entered and were shown to their seats by me on the right side and by MA on the left. Everybody seemed to sense that there was something odd; Ah, there were no Chinese waiters! Funny! . . . . The dinner commenced. There were to be no long speeches. My seven hands and seven of the MA's office started serving the high table. Our Ambassador asked me in a whisper, duly broadcast by the concealed loud speakers; *"What's happening? Why are you serving?* Answer: *All's well. Tell you later.* Our Prime Minister (PM): *Kya horahā hai?*[50] Answer: *Sab theek hogaya hai; bād mé batāoounga".* The Reverend Lama's, Dalai and Panchen, both in their late teens, seem delighted. They rose in their seats to thank me each time I served them. So too, Mao Chu Shi (*Chu Shi* = *Chairman*) and Premier Chou said, *Shiéh, shiéh* (thank you) each time. So far all

---

[50] ***PM:*** *Kya horahāhai? What's happening? Answer: Sab theek hogāya hai;* All's well ; *bād mé batāoounga I shall tell you later* "

went well. So, I thought. We had no menu cards. Heavens! Opar Singh entered with his menu card on his beard, a bit of Jilebi! Obviously, Opar had made sure that his Jilabies tasted good. He dodged the MA and made his way to the VVIP table and served from his dish. Dinner ended on the dot of 8 p.m. VVIPs and VIPs, and all normal human beings, except the Servers left. Dead tired, we just dropped onto empty chairs in the hall; there was hardly any Indian food left; the bathtub was empty. Plenty of Chinese food was available. MA and I wanted to take it easy; others started eating. Hardly 15 minutes after the Hall had emptied, there was the din of motorcycles in front of the hotel. A Chinese Military Officer, possibly of Brigadier Rank, saluted me, *"Chairman Mao greets you; he awaits you in Tien An Men. Take your time we shall accompany you."*

Too tired to eat, I was ready to go. All of us, Diplomatic Officers, who had been invited, immediately got into our cars, accompanied by Chinese Military Motorbikes on either side of us, in a regular motorcade. We reached Tien An Men and entered the hall. We were told that a whole line of seats for us invitees had been reserved in the second row, immediately behind the VVIPs. My seat and my wife's were immediately behind Chairman Mao and our PM. As soon as we were spotted and about to sit, Mao Chu Shi stood up. He bowed to us. In Chinese,—later translated to me—he said*"Indian hospitality is something that we should copy. This is the first time that Diplomats have shown what diplomacy is. All service is praiseworthy. China thanks you. Please enjoy yourselves."* We did enjoy ourselves. No wonder I recall the **Diplomatic Dinner**. One happy consequence I shall dwell upon anon.

———————————

Minister Chou En Lai did attend the meeting of the Quartet in Bandung. He was to have travelled in an Indian plane, the Kashmir Princess, specially put at his disposal. Fortunately, he changed his plans at the last moment. He must have been forewarned. Mysteriously, the Princess disappeared near Borneo. All our investigations pointed to sabotage.

Was it in SEATO's interest that Chou should not be in Bandung?

There are few ironclad rules of diplomacy but to one there is no exception. When an official reports that talks were useful, it can safely be concluded that nothing was accomplished.
John Kenneth Galbraith

VIGNETTE 27. HEADY COCKTAIL

Twenty years of diplomatic life had been sources both of In-formation and Education for us, man, wife and Jeeves (Gopalan). We were in Shanghai towards the end of the tenure. My Consul General ship in Shanghai was ending in mid-1969. We were throwing, we thought, our final cocktail before weighing anchor. Nearly all our acquaintances, friends, diplomatic colleagues and fellow Indians were our guests.

Our abode was a duplex flat of the two topmost floors of the tallest skyscraper **Shih Pa Lo** (18 floors) with extensive open-air patios, one, the smaller beside the dining room, the size of one badminton court, and the other outside the drawing room of a tennis court. We could have entertained in the open-air alone, some 400 guests and within the drawing room at least a 100, the dining room being left for the "short-eats" and long drinks.

Shih Pa Lo was built some 50 years earlier by the Sassoon family of Mumbai. They were opium traders and lived in the international zone. A large number of white Russians, mostly Jewish, and highly cultured occupied the other floors. They were compelled to remain in China till the foreign companies in which they were working had settled their accounts and what China claimed was due to them because they had not paid taxes, Shanghai being in the international zone. Similarly, several Parsees from India had also close associations with the then Governments and Trading Houses of foreigners. My wife and I made a point of looking after a Parsee club and graveyard because there was no Tower of Silence. For the Jews, I used to help by getting them the basic necessities for worship in their Synagouges. Incidentally, the great Siegfried Sassoon, the poet was a nephew of the Sassoon's. Looking straight out from our duplex, was the biggest hotel of 4 floors; to the left was the French Club; to the right, the race course.

The Indian Consul General's cocktails were never to be missed: you had to cut dinner; and even supper would be quite unnecessary. The cocktail was for normally 1 to 2 hours, 6pm to 8.Invitees were expected to start leaving by 7:30.

Our guests included: Shanghai Chinese Foreign Office Officials, nearly a dozen of them; Heads of other Consulate Generals and Consulates with wives; the equivalent of the Mayor of Shanghai; almost all the couples living in Shih Pa Lo; chief Indian citizens in Shanghai and, of course, all our Senior Staff numbering 6 couples. Of other important citizens of various races, there would have been at least 25 couples including Russian Jews who had fled Russia before it became Communist and some who had came from other parts of China before it became Communist. Many guests had been heads of firms from Australia and USA. Actually, therefore, the Indian cocktails were unique because they were glorious opportunities to meet interesting people whom they would not otherwise have not even known each other. Other countries' Missions in Shanghai did not enjoy our non-aligned status.

Our cocktail party had already had all invitees enjoying themselves by 6:30 p.m. There was a telephone call and our Chinese cook answered it. He entered in a hurry and told me that some Chinese VIP was on the phone and requested me to spare a moment for him. I duly hurried and asked who was speaking and what I could do for him?

In French, *"Don't you recognize my voice ?"*
Self: *"Not quite. But it's familiar"*
Voice: *"Chou En-Lai"*
Self: *"Good day. Where are you speaking from?"*
C: *"From the hotel in front of your building. I am told you are having a party. I have not been invited".*
Self: *"You don't need an invitation. You know that my home belongs to you. When you are coming I shall be waiting for you, downstairs."*
C: *"On no account downstairs. May I came with a couple of my companions? We shall be there within 10 minutes."*
Self: *"Thank you very much. My wife will be delighted".*

Our conversation was in French.

Immediately, I was told by Gao, our Chinese cook, that the whole building entrances and exits had been guarded. I told my wife what was to happen mentioning the name of the distinguished guest. The whole crowd present were agog. The Diplomats were astounded. Never had such a thing happened. What a co-incidence!

Premier Chou En-Lai were received by my wife and me at the lift-door. I had the honour of being in parties given by Premiers but never had been a host to any one of them. He knew French having been in France, quite a time in his younger days. He was completely at ease. He told me that he was happy that I had such a variety of fellow guests. The USSR Consul General was amazed and so was the whole Consular Corps.

As soon I knew that Premier Chou was coming I sent for his favorite drink, *Mau Tai*, which is something like vodka. Either I or my wife were with him throughout. It was amazing how friendly he was. He ate short eats casually. Jeeves Gopalan, rose to the occasion and cooked up something special. The Premier was delighted. It was past the zero hour of 8 p.m. No one departed. At last, nearing 9 p.m., Premier Chou took his leave, telling me that the evening was most useful to him and recalled the Diplomatic Dinner of 1954, October in Peking.

Our Ambassador in Peking was, of course, informed by me as well as our HQ in New Delhi. I learnt later that a non-IFS Officer took my place. The Consul General's residence was shifted, I think to the Chancery.

Shanghai had been for me a great, and as it happened, a welcome change. Of course it was an independent charge and hence I was freer to operate than in Peking. Leaving Shanghai was a wrench; but when is it not a wrench anywhere to leave people whom we have got to know and like; lovely sights we saw and admired; Hangchow, Soochow, Nanching, Hofei, ... Farewell, China.

I felt, a decade later, happier for having been in China when I became Commissioner in Hong Kong and able the better to fulfil my duties there. I welcome the rendition of China's territory which took place duly before the end of 20th Century.

MUSINGS

Vignette 28. Pilgrim's Progress

Brāhmanical Journey

At the end of 20th century, has the World 'progressed' beyond **Primaevality**? Or, have we regressed? The trite but perennial and persistent debate about what Progress is, remains undetermined. Of course, Change has been abundant, even breath-taking. Generally, Peoples everywhere, think that they have either broken away from bonds, or that they are freer from the most constricting; or, at least, that there is a scent of Freedom. But this scent evaporates eftsoons. Famines have been less severe, be it in Ethiopia, Saharan Africa or elsewhere. In populous East and South Asia, Hunger is no longer the prime plague. Yet, *plus ça change plus ça reste la meme*[51],People still "remain, on the brink of pain." Consequently they seek transitory Pleasure. It soon collects its lethal toll. There is no Joy, no Bliss. Why?

One is compelled to re-define 'Progress'. Most catholically it is approach towards a goal. But goals differ; not only from one part of the Globe to another, but from group to group, family to family, individual to individual. Obviously, it is not possible, nor even desirable to homogenise mankind as religions and politicians attempt to do and fail. Why did and why do they fail? Because, the perceptions of the leaders themselves vary from person to person, from time to time. Soon differences are called heresy or blasphemy; they provoke persecution and retaliation. Eventually, old Orders break down, whether or not new ones replace them. Result, chaos.

Progress ought to lead to contentment, at least for a time. Contentment too is brought about in different people by different or even opposite means. That leaves us almost where we were at the outset. Almost, but not quite. We must might persist in our enquiry. The only way to obtain contentment, or **Nirvana,** or **Moksha,** or Salvation, is to

---

[51]   **plus ça change . . .:** *the more it changes the more it is the same.*

seek it within oneself. Withdrawal is Detachment. The ardent do not like this; particularly many socially conscious Indians—they may be generically dubbed Indo-Anglians—ascribe almost convincingly, the miseries around us in India to political subjugation of the country, and its fissuring into centrifugal units and apathy, to indolence and to tolerance of intolerance. The latter, the actors, and the former, Contemplators, do not need, however, to be mutually hostile, intolerant or exclusive: there are a sufficient number of "Actors" to suffer "Contemplators." Contemplators are scarcely perturbed by the 'Actors" impatience. If such a mix were not there, India would not remain India; then there would have been no need for "Freedom" from aliens, English and, earlier, Mongol Rulers.

The answer, surely, is that everyone attains his goal in his own way. The wish to thwart others is ineffective. In India, with its extent, its demographic variety, its long history of habitation, its natural wealth having been drawn upon continuously, obviously, the unique way is to follow one's conscience without acrimony. There is enough room, in the World as a whole, and in the Indian part of it, to conquer oneself, become kinder, gentler, universal rather than fanatic, fractious, rough and opinionated. Act then, as character impels without harshly undermining others. But Act; do not be inactive or merely restive. The true **Hindu (=Indian** of any faith) is guided by: the Vedas, Zend Avesta, Tripittaka, Old and the New Testaments of the Bible, Koran, Granth Sahib, Analects, Tao De Ching, Tirukkural. The Peripatetic and the Stagirite; Stoic and Epicure; Calvin and Bahaullah, Tagore, Aurobindo, Ramakrishna Paramahamsa, Ramana Maharshi, Gandhi, Marx, Russel, Lavoisier, Darwin, Rutherford, Huxley, Niels Bohr, Einstein, Bose, Raman, Bhabha, Radhakrishnan are all Seers of different aspects of the proverbial Elephant for 'wise men of Hindoostan.'

Progress, for all true *Hindu(=*Indians), the Cosmos-Conscious, is, therefore:

(i) *Intrinsic evolution from within.*

This means greater use of the grey cells, of which we presently activate but a negligible fraction, and of which most of us will use even less if we be enslaved by gadgetry that increasingly circumscribes our lives, makes robots of diversely thinking men and women, boys and girls. Bio-engineering and cybernetics, unharnessed, will even bring forth patterned and lifelong infants. This is proved by contemporary industrially, over-developing robot society.

(ii) *Acquisition of greater power and prowess,* possibly through **Yoga** or **Tai Ch'hi Ch'huan**: the ability to cast one's mind into space, to communicate without words or gestures, in utter silence, and even at a distance.

(iii) *Cultivation of Empathy and Equanimity:* ***Aum, Shāntih.***

(iv) *Realisation of Oneness in Infinity. Conquering the Ego.*

These ends are not being gained now; indeed, we are distancing ourselves from them, yielding to short term economic compulsions; for, even fame and skill in pastimes, even spiritual guidance, are all now marketed. Unleashed Technocracy has induced an alibi for intrinsic progress. Change becomes extrinsic. Our environment may improve, even that is unsure; but Man is certainly decaying patently. If, therefore, Technology does not cease to be the Tyrant, it already is, its despotism will destroy itself. This will perhaps be wrought, ironically, by the very economic forces by which Technology is motored. The ***Atharvana Veda***, (Applied Science) which has become the chief instrument and catalyst for material change may be relegated to neglect. The amenities of Technology will be appropriately and selectively, availed of. The intrinsic potency of the Individual will again be developed; Man will **Progress.**

We all want progress, but if you're on the wrong road, progress
means doing an about-turn and walking back to the right road;
in that case, the man who turns back soonest
is the most progressive.

C. S. Lewis

Vignette 29. Gender et al

Emancipation is defined as freedom from restraint and, so, "progressive!" Yet, absolutely, it would be regressive: Restraint was the key to the door of civilization. It enabled orderly evolution. That idea, which led man to being humane and cease being bestial, was that of self-restraint from promiscuity: most women and many men, particularly the *sattwik,* virtuous and pure, restrained and restricted themselves to a single partner, hopefully for life. Marriage, far more climacterically than the wheel, distinguished primaeval mankind from the primitive. Conjugal aberration was deplored; concepts of legitimacy and illegitimacy gestated in society individual responsibility of father for offspring; and child's love for father was born; paternal guidance and example complemented maternal care; to these joint familial responsibility was the complement. The consequence was efflorescence of culture and self-assurance. The family provided insurance against calamity and vicissitude. The Oekonomia was founded upon Faith, Hope and Charity, which other institutions, from ecclesia to socialism, strove to substitute, with disastrous consequences manifest by the contemporary plight of most of the nearly 6 billion human beings, and billion billion other forms of life. The Joint Family, Sinic and Indic, evolved economical, collaborative and co-operative ways of life. Surrender of egotism was the premium for insurance policies for life, from conception to the observance of death anniversaries. Awareness and appreciation of corporate and communal living permitted spiritual evolution into unselfishness and platonic affection for all life.

The *leit motif* of the suffragettes was "equality" or even "identity" of male and female. It is a consequence of the Industrial and French Revolutions combined: they had shattered, in Europe, the concept of the Joint Family, giving it a bad name by calling it "feudal" and promptly guillotining it. The myth of "progress" was a concoction of greed, capitalism and pretended concern for universal happiness. Suffrage, emancipation, equality were slogans whose unique intent was to generate and increase dividends. Competition created pandemonium; monopoly was born of marriages of convenience called mergers. Life has been come consequently a Rake's Progress[52].

> *"For what wears our life of mortal men?*
> *'Tis that from change to change their being rolls;*
> *'Tis that repeated shocks, again, again,*
> *Exhaust the energy of strongest souls,*
> *And numb the elastic powers,*
> *Till having us'd our nerves with bliss and teen,*
> *And tired upon a thousand schemes our wit,*
> *To the just-pausing Genius we remit*
> *Our worn-out life, and are—what we have been.*
>
> **Matthew Arnold ex**
> **Scholar Gipsy.**

Crusades against Gender Exploitation, Child Abuse, Sweated Labour and, presently, the Gadarene plunge into ephemeral "Webs" and "Internets" of endless imitation are no quests for Grails of Happiness for All: they are smoke screens that hide the armada that craves despotic wealth. Hope of happiness is the *ignis fatuus* that inveigles man into the quicksands of Time. That hope is baulked, is doomed.

> *Thou waitest for the spark from Heaven: and we,*
> *Vague half-believers of our casual creeds,*
> *Who never deeply felt, nor clearly will'd,*
> *Whose insight never has borne fruit in deeds,*
> *Whose weak resolves never have been fulfill'd;*
> *For whom each year we see*
> *Breeds new beginnings, disappointments new;*
> *Who hesitate and falter life away,*
> *And lose to-morrow the ground won today-*
>
> **-idem**

---

[52] **Rake's Progress:** *This term has been virtually coined by the mid-18th century English painter Hogarth's series of five paintings illustrating the decay of Man.*

And Arnold prophesies:

> *This strange disease of modern life,*
> *With its sick hurry, its divided aims,*
> *Its heads o'ertax'd. Its palsied hearts . . . .*

idem

It is obvious to those Indians who set some store by their independence of thought, to Indians who are not "flies to the wanton gods" of cyber space, to Indians inspired by Aurobindo and Ramana Maharshi, to Indians who have not booked seats on the Rake's Progress Express to the world of Detroit, that the contemporary Revolution leads to Gulags, to Hiroshima's, to My-laise. Far better is a "Pilgrimage to our Source", in physical decrepitude to plod to Badri Nath, Kedar Nath, Vaishnava Devi in "natural piety" to be one with **ALL**, the Infinite.

Brāhminical thought is based on the premise of the Cycles of Rebirths. It is the premise too of Mahāvira, Buddha, Guru Nānak, Nārayaṇa Guru, the Saï Bābā's; they truly represent Indianness, placing no faith in political Ballot Boxwālāhs' assertions of equitable Societies.

The regard, in which women and the so-called deprived communities had been held, was deliberately denied; aspersions were cast on caste by would-be "convertors". Regard is now replaced by apathy; soon it will engender antipathy, were pilgrimage to our source is not undertaken.

Fatuous is the suffragette upon the Indian scene. She cuts a ludicrous figure; sexexploitation is brazenly flaunted on Stage and Ramp and Hustings. Non—entities are heads of political parties. In the Vote Slave-market vulgar display of daughters and sons is nauseous to any thinking Indian. Thought is stymied by the updated Bread and Circuses, sops to the Cerberus, of commercialized Ramps, Beauty Parades and Parlours, dens of cacophonic parody of music, encouragement to discard standards, morals, self-control. Crocodile tears are shed over "abuses" of Gender *et al* meticulously sponsored by cynical mass-media.

Vignette 30. School Gurukula

Teaching Spouses

The "**REMOVE**[53]," Stds. XI and XII, the last two years of Pre-University Schooling, can be beneficent or maleficent. Its influence, with accent on evolving the sprouting intellect and burgeoning body, used to depend upon parental environment. Nowadays, the deracination of World Youth from the original natural setting, the Village, and virtual extinction of the Joint and the Extended Families, is the chief reason for maladjustments and desperate quests for excitement followed by anodynes. Indian youth, especially from affluent, upper-middle and many middle-middle class economic and cultural families are prone to succumb to the Dis-Ease called "modernity." The World, including India, is in a maelstrom of protean values.

India is an excellent laboratory for the evolution of youth, both male and female. Its ageing variety, unstaled by Custom, enables it to evolve a remedy which could help all Peoples. Schools should find in "**REMOVES**," the remedy for these "lean and pursy times." As always, the cure is reversion to the original GURUKULA, the familial abode of learning. Not much heeded is the latter component of the term: **Kula**. It means Family.

Abodes of Learning must become homes. This is because of economic and, sometimes, social ways of living. In nuclear families, the mother-housewife is absent as long as the father is; Home is left to servants who are not, as they used to be, members of the family, sometimes called *retainers,* belonging to generations living together. Such retainers are no longer available. The home is left to casual labour or to companies running domestic services. They have to employ bands of workers who, necessarily, can have contact with those for whom they

---

[53] "*Remove*" *is the technical term used for the period between the usual end of schooling, Standards X and the University, viz., Standards XI and XII.*

are sent to work. When children, in their latter teens return home from study at the same time as they used to do before "*removing*, "have to open empty homes with duplicate keys. Rarely do they find Mummy or Daddy. When they do come, both are tired out. The son or daughter has to fend for himself or herself; having a sibling is becoming uncommon. Parent couples find it difficult to cope even with a single offspring. It follows, therefore, the "**REMOVE**" must be a home; not monastery or convent. Both *Purusha and Prakriti*, male and female, are essential. Their Foster Parents, both teaching spouses, set the example, living and growing in harmony. Such environment will have a profound effect on values of later teenagers. We are now suffering because of the absence of such an environment. Co-educational **Removes** would have couples of teacher foster parents, in separate houses on the same campus at, say, the eastern and western ends. Dormitories would be on the first floor. The foster parents would live on the ground floor.

It would be marvellous if the sets of foster parents of the **Remove** could teach different subjects, thus covering the greater part of the Courses. It would be splendid if there were also grandparents; the teaching couple would be the freer to update themselves. No servants are needed for the dormitories as the students must learn how to fend for themselves.

Being in the school campus, the students would entertain themselves with the many amenities provided within the campus. No time will be wasted in commuting. The whole School would benefit. At times, when there are brief shortages of teachers, the "**Removers**" could be stand-bys. (**Āchāryā Vidya Kula** (AVK) has often had to have recourse to this ploy,—with excellent results). School Timetables would be adjusted so that plus-two teachers meld into one academic team. Enhanced by the presence of the more qualified staff, all aspects of the school would benefit.

During children's latter teens, teachers' and students' concerns will also be intellectual, moral, ethical and metaphysical. This will be catered to, conclusively in the first of the two years: XI Std. It will complete the attempt which should have been made in their VIII Std., before concern with their Final School Examination overwhelms them. The foster parents of the Remove will take cognizance of this; the Dharmamananam classes of when they were aged 12 to 13 will be complemented. The "Removers" would be told about the *Sathvik* Age for which they should prepare themselves if only to pass on to their progeny, the Idea of the

Supreme goal, *Sat Chit Anandam* (Infinite Bliss). The Alumni will then be members of the virtual Kibbutz[54] which should form the Sathvik Society. Their **Remove** will be the model for the Kibbutzim in the last quarter of this very century.

Brāhmanically, to deal with the problem of Education all over the world is relatively easy in the human laboratory that India is. Because of its being a terrestrial microcosm, its variety of race, language and religion as well as political thinking, enables it to evolve a suitable method, applicable all over the World. Our problem is that contemporary youth is now *in-ducated* and not *e-ducated*. The culprit is the Leviathan State. It has bureaucratized, stultified indoctrinated. Ecclesiae started the rot by catechizing 'Lambs of the Flock'.

The State is now egged on by Beelzebub (Satan's right hand man): Commercialism. Along with it, misused technology is converting youth into machines, *robotniki*. Industry has become inorganic, despoiling the Earth. A not so Brave New World is begot by mis-application of Science, deplorably creating "sepulchres of crime." Schools and Universities profess philanthropy, but turn out, on their conveyor belts, mindless and thoughtless technicians and technocrats. Even in the Humanities, States dictate curricula. They make children mere tape-recorders of 'facts', most of them irrelevant in later life. When their alumni begin to know more and more of less and less in the name of "Specialization."

The obvious remedy is to re-humanize teaching. It can be effectively done by removing Education from the purview of the centralizing State, and entrusting it once again to Teachers, *"full men,"* as Bacon would term them. A *"full Man"* or *"full Woman"* is one who is happy, contented,

---

[54] ***Kibbutz:*** *Israel has Kibuttzim which preceded its re-formation. In Kibuttzim (pl), the structure of the whole Judaic society was reproduced and their ideals concretely shown. This enabled true democracy to take roots, in most cases in Kibuttzim, all amenities were in common. They proved themselves so strong that the British who were mandatory governing Palestine could not resist the strength of the Kibuttzim. They and their likes, to this day, maintained harmoniously their immediate independence as well as uphold the authority of the State as a whole, whereas the Soviet Communist Kolkhozes failed. In fact, in the outskirts of many cities of the USA, the Jews have created Kibuttzim which provides for all their needs. The most sophisticated technological aids are available so that the Jewish lobby is the most disciplined and powerful in the US Oekonmoeia.*

domestic, industrious, economic and ready to learn. Normally, only married couple qualify: they not merely raise but also rear children. During the evolution of Society, the initial civilizing factor was not the Wheel but Marriage: preferably monogamous, permissibly polygamous, never polyandrous, never Free Loving, Concubinant or "Gay." The family is the microcosm to the macrocosmic World Society. Countries, termed Nations, are passing political clouds, ephemera. The permanent unit is the Family. Hence, it is the Tutorial Couple that is the justification and *raison* d'être of Public Schooling. They provide the natural ambience that modern life denies to youth. Tutors have scores of ideal models, their precursors: Bhrigu, Valmiki, Seneca, Lao-Tze, Confucius . . . . Necessarily, the Tutor must master his/her discipline. Aristotle-wise, but he or she must also be profoundly Platonic. Spouses, would both be complementary and supplementary. More important it is in Schools, especially the REMOVE for the 16 to 18 year olds, that their Homes should be ideal, neither austere nor garish; simple yet not bare; aesthetic but not arty or Bohemian; disciplined not puritan. The truth should never be hidden or even camouflaged. When questions are considered brazen, prurient or embarrassing, answers may be postponed, never denied.

Both foster parents should exemplary, be, themselves, students with a passion for self-improvement and experiment; they should manifestly love each other and their wards; be industrious, eschew servants and make the foster-family part of the KIBBUTZ. A perfect co-ed residential school should be in or near rural surroundings, part of a self-sufficient and self-reliant economy. It must rely on solar heating, bio-gas, ground-water and herbal medicine. Water should be recycled; bio-control, vermicultured compost be used so that their KIBBUTZ becomes independent; a free republican Panchayat with equitable allocation of duties. Entertainment should be 'live', not capsuled. Celebrities may be occasionally invited. Imported or recorded amusement should be minimal.

It may be objected that such a scenario is: (a) too Utopian, and (b) poor preparation for the contemporary urbanized World. The rebuttal is that if such education turns the alumni or alumnae away from putrefaction, so much the better; for, the present trend of the world is suicidal. May apostolic alumni reconstruct life in Kibbutzim. These would consist not only of scholars: most would cater to other needs; musical, artisanal, hand manufacturing, food conserving, carpet weaving, footwear making, hand looming, or whatever. Such hamlets will restore the Auburns where 'Accumulated Wealth has decayed men'. There is no other way out of the labyrinth. Gandhiji was right. Nehru was wrong. The ideal pair, tutor and spouse, would be Goldsmith's Schoolmaster in the **Deserted Village;** or his depiction of himself as **Vicar of Wakefield.**

This land, India, fortunately, has an increasing number of youths who would happily become isotopes or alchemists making dross into gold. The ideal INDIAN High School will be today's philosopher's stone to convert our *nakli* (nickel) currency[55] back to *asli* gold the *Mahātmic way.*

> *I have come to believe that a great teacher is a great artist and that*
> *there are as few as there are any other great artists.*
> *Teaching might even be the greatest of the arts since the medium is*
> *the human mind and spirit.*
>
> *John Steinbeck*

---

[55] ***Nakli* Currency:** *the silver Indian rupee even after World War II was* ₹ *13.5= £I. When £ I was nearly 10gms of gold. By 2000 A.C 1 £ =* ₹ *80. I£* became worth less than its purchasing value by 90%. By 2013 10gms of gold was not ₹13.5 but ₹30,000. India had a credit balance in £ of £, $ and Swiss Francs. This shows that the purchasing power parity (PPP) of the ₹ has shrunk to almost 1/100th of its original value. Currency is an accepted measuring rod the World over. To pretend that wonderful giant technology as brought prosperity to Indians is not tenable, to put it mildly.

Vignette 31. Metaphysical Alchemist

The unsullied mind is my crucible,
Reason the litmus, judgment the balance.
I accept tentatively the credible,
Renounce definitely all dalliance
With hypnotic Belief.
No bond-slave am I, despairing, submitting,
To yoke my free-thinking,
I am Indian brave enough to think;
Myself to invoke **Antaryamin,**
The Influence, evoking **Antarjyothi,**
The re-membered flame.
God recalled by yet another name.
I would not by religion e'er be bound;
I would by Metaphysic myself reclaim,
Free, discriminating.
All around I hear the noisy clank
Of rusting chains of faiths,
Fettering obsequious followers
Hamstrung, manacled, numbed,
Atrophied brains,
Chain-ganged shibboleth-swallowers,
And mis-appliéd Science followers
Spent in labyrinthine pains.
Particles are we all of Cosmic Thought
Unraveling riddles of mythologists.
Self-assured, we would not be caught
In the webs of self-seeking Theologists,
Archbishops, Mullahs, Lamas, Popes,
Who one day may perhaps Enlighten themselves;
But vain are their hopes

If their pronunciamentos
Are meant to frighten intelligent thinkers
Into anodyned submission
By Encyclicals sans remission
And Ecumenicals conjuring intermission.

Makara Sankranti 1990

Vignette 32. Humour

English distinguishes itself from other languages by the important role it gives to **Humour,** not least in Oratory. French prefers **Wit;** German, **Militancy;** Italian, **Mellifluity;** Urdu, hyperbolical **Politeness;** Persian, **Flight of Fancy;** Chinese, **Oriental Inscrutability.** Demosthenes' **Philippics**[56] would have not been appreciated in London's Houses of Commons or Lords: because they are humourless. The most cutting points in English are made by pre-eminent parliamentarians in the House of Commons because of their Punch Effect[57]. Oxford and Cambridge

---

[56] **Philippics:** *Demosthenes is the most famous orator of the Greco-Roman world. He had great defects in speech. Nevertheless, he developed in his early twenties, an overwhelming desire to orate and become famous. A stammering and stuttering orator would not be considered one. His well meaning friends dissuade him. He was obstinate and determined. He went to the seashore, picked up some smoothened pebbles and put them in his mouth, and,* **Eureka***! his pronunciation and enunciation gradually improved. He persisted and overcame all his defects; in addition, he out-roared the waves. Nowadays, he would have needed no loudspeaker. His* **'Phillipics'** *were against Philip of Macedon who was bent upon conquering the whole of Hellas, the Greek world; His son, Alexander the Great (?), did finally achieve even more. Philip, as a conquering emperor decided upon making an Imperial Progress, mounted on a stallion through the richest victim city of Hellas, Corinth. The streets were lined with the enslaved and sullen mob. His progress was dignified and slow. An old hag sate herself precariously on a sloping, tiled roof. As Philip progressed, proudly nose in air on his mount, he passed just below her. She was armed. She had a tile pulled out from beneath her seat; she hurled it at Philip. He dropped, a corpse. She had avenged the death of her son in the glorious victory. Destiny reserved a similar fate for the great son who died shivering of a fever on his return from India in the Persian desert.*

[57] **PUNCH:** *A Weekly also called* **Charivari.** *Over a century, it was mental dessert which English Gentlemen most enjoyed. Alas!* **Punch** *Rests in Peace. Was*

produced many Members of Parliament (MPs), whose orations were effective. Even non-Ox-Cam's spiced their jargon to provoke laughter-inducing pleasure, thereby preventing animosity. Our Indian Hon. MPs, copying English Houses, but lacking humour, end up with fisticuffs, certainly not entertaining, actually demeaning.

Ox-Cam Unions' debates are participated by teenagers speaking to fellow members of the Union which is meant for budding scholars. An excellent Library, comfortable drawing room, superb canteen create *bonhomie.* University Professors, and Lecturers with such an upbringing, automatically made their speeches, not only profound, but also entertaining. Not only did wit induce smiles, their humour provoked guffaws. We shall conclude with the experience of two Indian undergraduates, both members of the Oxford Union and the Oxford Majlis (Society of Indian undergrads).

A revered Indian of our time was Fellow of **All Souls,** a college meant solely for distinguished, Scholars who pursued their own profound studies. If they wished, they could guide post-graduate alumni of Oxford and also give series of Lectures.

One such scholar was an Indian; his Fellowship was for a term, and he was making his *début as a lecturer.* He was to become world famous for more than his Scholarship. We Indians were understandably proud of him for having become Fellow of ALL Souls.

Our learned Indian Pandit, started his lecture to a full hall overflowing into the corridor. We were Indians from different colleges and different parts of India, with little knowledge of his metaphysical subject. We came early to seat ourselves both comfortably and modestly, in the centre of, not the first, but the second row. We identified ourselves as the speaker's countrymen by becoming the only one Brown ait in the White Sea. We occupied the same seats till the bi-weekly lectures were over.

The savant reached the lectern. After courteous bow and momentary deliberation, he spoke. The voice was sonorous; pauseless. He read from script; his eye never met any of the audience's. The lecture, even as it had started, ended on the dot. He bowed to us, the only two left after the hall had emptied. We returned the bow. All three went on several ways.

---

it because, too many Gentlemen have left Britain?

During his second lecture, we were more comfortable: the hall was only half-full. For the third lecture, it was three quarters empty; thereafter, only two seats were occupied by two brownies, the White Sea disappeared. The also brown orator, turbaned as usual was oblivious of his audience. It happened the exactly the same till the Finale. Not a laugh had interrupted the discourses. There was naught to smile about, let alone guffaw. Two brownies had proved their patriotism. For, if they hadn't been there, the lectures would have stopped. Oxford's usage was that, even if there was only one member in the audience, the series would not be discontinued. This had not happened in living memory. In fact, there had been not one but two of us!

Humourlessness was "cause" of the debacle[58]. The truly great scholar was Dr. Sarvepalli Radhakrishnan, the second President of India.

> *Humour is by far the most significant*
> *activity of the human brain.*
>
> *Edward de Bono*

---

[58] **DÉBACLE:** *Catastrophic failure. The speaker became very dear to me, my Icon. He was Shree. B.T. Keshava Iyengar (BTK), my father-in-law's friend, from their common youth in Mysore. He partook of midday meals in BTK's mother's house, once a week.In many middle-class Brahmins' homes, hospitality was extended to poorer Brahmin boys living in the same Agrahāra (quartier). They were called "**Week-boys**."*

Vignette 33. Shakespeare's Genius-I

Brāhmanic perspective

Shakespeare had me spellbound before teenage. I couldn't be critical, yet I felt uneasy after I left hallowed Oxford University. **Hamlet** was my favourite play and, in it, it was the character of the young Prince Hamlet. For the older King Hamlet, I gradually developed allergy. Already, in my early teens, the magic of Shakespeare's **diction** had me spellbound; not his **fiction**. His plots and characters are secondary and second hand. After Prince Hamlet, it was Julius Caesar followed by his very opposite, Falstaff, who were my favourite characters. Among the female characters it was Ophelia to whom I was most drawn, despite her tragically too brief an appearance in the play. I was most upset every time, I read about the final moments of Ophelia and Hamlet. I re-hearse words of Hamlet's mother.

> **Queen** : *Sweets to the sweet: farewell*
> *(scattering flowers) I hop'd thou shouldst have been my Hamlet's wife;*
> *I thought thy bride-bed to have deck'd, sweet maid, And not have strew'd*
> *thy grave.*

I confess that tears clouded my eyes because of what Shakespeare had done to them, so much against their own *Karma*. I found no inkling of evil in either of them. On the other hand, it was the father Hamlet who had caused all the mischief.

Shakespeare had yielded to the vogue for Revenge plays, which for a time were popular. Webster's **Duchess of Malfi** was a similar piece of injustice. Before we go further, let us reflect on the manner in which he wrote rather than the subject. He often put into the mouths of the secondary characters, magnificent blank verse which the character didn't deserve. For instance, Lorenzo's words about music reflected William Shakespeare's, not Lorenzo. It would have been more appropriate for Portia. Likewise, Theseus in the finale of **Midsummer Night's Dream**, when he talks about poetic genius, *'giving to airy nothing a local habitation* *and a name*, is again quite out of character of a warrior talking to his Amazonian wife. In other words, Shakespeare was not much interested in his characters. They were often hyperbolized.

Marlowe introduced to him, his *'mighty line'*, the Iambic pentameter. In it, Marlowe did not necessarily end-stop each verse; the dialogue is consequently closer to natural speech without, however, losing the musical effect of the Heroic Couplet of two Iambic rhyming pentameters. He also introduced the Heroic magniloquence, as in Tamburlane. Shakespeare had to use the Heroic Couplets, as also Marlowe, because, in contemporary practice, it ended important situations and scenes. It was not possible in the Elizabethan and Jacobian periods to have curtains for the Apron Stage, the rhyming couplet gave the signal of the end of the scene or at times end of an important speech.

Shakespeare was genial. He made up for lack of what he might have learned at the University in Latin, by being extremely popular with his fellow dramatists and actors. The Mermaid Tavern in London, not far from the theatres, was their tryst. All University Wits, Oxonian, and Cantabrian, used to meet there frequently. Shakespeare was obviously an excellent listener. The Wits' discourses included apart from wisdom, all figures of speech: hyperbole and litotes, metaphor and simile, couplets and blank verse, reason and rhyme, history and legend, both light and grave talk. The gossip obviously included references to various topics, past and contemporary. Therefore, Shakespeare's knowledge extended far beyond what he would have learned in his Stratford school.

Contemporary English political and social affairs were mirrored in his plays. England's great victory over the Spanish Armada (1588 AC) and Francis Drake's incursion into Spanish waters had great effect upon English nationalism. This included idolization of English pirates, looting the precious cargo of the Spanish galleons from Mexico and Peru. The loot reached not Madrid but London or Plymouth. The last ten years of the Virgin (?) Queen Elizabeth (now called the First, because we have a second Elizabeth), and the first decade of James VIth of Scotland and Ist of England—1590 to 1610—mark the apogee of English literature. The descent from the apex started after the Versions were of the translated Bible authorized in 1611. This is important because Shakespeare and the King James' Bible, as it is called, marked the high water of English literature. It is an unequalled height, by a long chalk, let alone surpassed. Shakespeare and the Bible are referred to as 'Wells of English undefiled.'

The Bible had the advantage of having to be compulsorily read and explained strictly following ecclesiastical dictates, emanating from the Archbishops of Canterbury and York. They were second and third after the monarch. Henry VIII had taken the role of the Vatican Pope. He was no authority on the Bible or metaphysics. The other important fillip was that the Bible, including both the Testaments, Old and New, were in English, no longer Latin. Shakespeare would have been of the generation which attended, *de rigeur,* at least the Sunday services, since his teachers also were most probably connected with the Church and Sunday schools for children. He would be familiar with the entire mythology of the Bible. The other mythology with which he would be familiar was Greco-Latin, through Homer's **Iliad** and **Odyssey**, and Virgil's **Aeneid.** They would have been wells from which he drew inspiration.

Amongst Shakespeare's tragedies, I would put, in ascending order, **Othello, King Lear, Macbeth and Hamlet**. As for comedies they would be; **As You Like it, Midsummer Night's Dream, Tempest and Twelfth Night**. Metaphysically, the Tempest rises to great heights in which the chief character, Prospero, beautifully paraphrases Vedic thought:

> *Our revels now are ended. These our actors,*
> *As I foretold you, were all spirits and*
> *Are melted into air, into thin air:*
> *And, like the baseless fabric of this vision,*
> *The cloud-capp'd towers, the gorgeous palaces,*
> *The solemn temples, the great globe itself,*
> *Yea, all which it inherit, shall dissolve*
> *And, like this insubstantial pageant faded,*
> *Leave not a rack behind. We are such stuff*
> *As dreams are made on, and our little life*
> *Is rounded with a sleep.*

However, unlike Shankara, neither the great Omar Khayyam in his great **Rubaiyāt**, nor the great Shakespeare's Prospero tells us the why and wherefore and the whither the dreams lead, as we already know.

> *Māyam Idam Akhilam Buddhwā*
> *Brahmapadam prawishwa viddithwa*
> *(Having wisely learnt that all this is an illusion, follow that path*
> *which leads to Infinity)*

However, **Tempest** does not qualify as being the best of comedies because, apart from two dialogues, it is fantastic rather than imaginative. Whereas **Twelfth Night** is beautifully constructed and has far more humour, with wit well presented, whereas in **Tempest**, both with wit and humour reach their nadir.

I had a windfall. One of the apples which fell into my hand was about my icon, Shakespeare. The tree which dropped this apple was George Bernard Shaw (GBS), whom you shall duly meet.

I asked GBS a question which I thought would be naïve on my part. It was, "*As a playwright, what do you feel about my icon, William Shakespeare? Do you think with Ben Jonson, that he really is 'not of an age, but of all time.'* GBS said, '*The trouble is he didn't know how to write plays. Just compare him to me. I leave you to ponder over this.*"

I pondered. My icon was far too dear to me for him to be toppled from my altar. It was only when I began teaching English literature that the pondering conceived the Idea. I examined play after play, including my most beloved **Hamlet** which was my '*preicious Perl Withouten Spotte*' (Middle English Pearl about the poet's late daughter). The idea matured. It confirmed that it couldn't possibly have been Francis Bacon who was the author of Shakespeare's works. Shakespeare was cast among those like Marlowe who had been to a University. As a good listener and chum of the Wits, confirmed by Ben Jonson, he would have, no doubt, learnt about the sources for the plots of his plays. But he was not at all critical about them. He felt it is his religious duty to adhere, as far as possible, to what had been written by authors Italian, French, Spanish . . . . Consequently, he put together a *pot pourré* (*kichidi or goulache*), regardless of the roles of the characters in his plays. He used dialogues for them which were out of character with their roles. Their mouths were fountains for his divine Blank Verse.

For example: in **Merchant of Venice**, Lorenzo and Jessica, are neither of them remarkable. The former is an unimpressive bride snatcher of a young girl with plenty of stolen jewels and cash; the latter, a lonely child, obviously motherless, with an oaf of a servant to keep her company. Quite out of character, the couple broadcasts to the audience, some of the finest words on music in English literature. Similarly, in **Antony and Cleopatra**, Enobarbus is given unforgettable lines about Cleopatra, lines which '*age has not withered nor custom staled its infinite variety.*' Nothing else that Enobarbus is made to say gives an inkling of such richness. Likewise, the Old Duke **in As You Like it,** makes his one great speech, as it were, tongue-in-cheek, **on** Adversity. His Jacques too is given lovely blank verse for his Seven Ages, as though he were a superficial observer, instead of a budding metaphysician as he was cast. One reason was that many of the actors of these parts were his Boon-Companions; he could not deny them each a good speech. Even bringing in the caskets in the **Merchant of Venice,** despite good verse metrically, is too far-fetched. The fact was that Shakespeare did not wish to mould his themes to proper shape, nor reject triviality. But he was a wizard with language. Macbeth's soliloquy, his last, starting '*Tomorrow and Tomorrow* . . . .' is superb. In between, Macbeth, apart from good soliloquies, he is not much of a character; a fine soldier, but a hen-pecked and infatuated fool of a husband.

Vignette 34. Shakespeare's Genius-II

Hamlet–Brāhmanised

What pains me most is Shakespeare's treatment of Hamlet and Ophelia. These two characters are my constant companions and fill my few vacant hours. The villain in **Hamlet** is definitely not the worthless Claudius. It is Hamlet, the king father of the prince. As a ghost, he should never have been let out of Hell or Hades or Purgatory as the then Christians allowed him to be. He asked his only and dear (?) son to take Revenge, a most un-Christian thing to do, seeing that Almighty God would do the needful. It is certainly a most un-Brāhmanical thing to do! Poor Shakespeare had to yield to money-making popularity of his contemporary audience and the current fashion for Revenge plays. He strewed the stage with corpses and the memory with four more: Polonius, lovely Ophelia and the two charlatan's Rosencrantz and Gildenstern, merely to sate his audience for silver pennies. The result was disastrous.

Father Hamlet gave no thought to the fact that wicked brother Claudius would be doomed to endless punishment in Hell. Instead, he goads his ideal son, one of the finest of characters, to death; he would have made a much better Monarch and a happy one with his Ophelia. In the event, Hamlet died unshriven even as the father had been; his Queen, whom he professed to adore, drinks a goblet of wine, poisoned by Claudius, meant for the Prince. The old man wanted Hamlet to avenge his death without being shriven. He sends Hamlet out of the world in exactly the same condition, unshriven. Not only does Hamlet die by being cheated in a duel with a poisoned and unblunted rapier, Laertes, who would have been esteemed brother-in-law of Hamlet's, is himself killed. Denmark becomes the kingdom of Fortinbras, son of the very man whom King Hamlet had killed. Polonius, Ophelia's father, was also done to death by an accident brought about by Claudius. Ophelia dies of grief, maddened, because he had been killed by her beloved Hamlet. We then hear of deaths of two courtiers, Rosencrantz and Gildenstern—though we may feel that they fully deserved to be executed, for the betrayal of their fellow student, Prince Hamlet.

Polonius was mistakenly killed behind the curtain by Hamlet who thought it was Claudius. Polonius was eaves-dropping behind the curtain at the instance of Claudius to overhear Hamlet and his mother's conversation. Sweet Ophelia whom Shakespeare, painted so lovingly in his immortal words, still haunts me. She was so woe-stricken that she became a lunatic, stepping into a stream full of lilies, gradually sinking and breathing her last. A lovely bud which never opened.

Were I to rewrite the Play, I would have dispensed with Claudius by his mistakenly drinking the goblet of wine poisoned by himself. I would have avoided poisoning Laertes' rapier. I would also allow Polonius merely to have fainted after a kick by Hamlet and imprisoned by Claudius, lest he betray him. Of course, Shakespeare's groundlings would not have been satisfied with a single corpse, Claudius'.

After all, having pondered Shaw's remark, I see that he was right. Shakespeare was not at all concerned about aught else but hypnotizing words and too faithful adherence to the source of his plays. It was alright with Plutarch but not with others'.

I would have then called Hamlet an ingenious Romantic Tragi-Comedy.

> *Life's but a walking shadow, a poor player, that struts*
> *and frets his hour upon the stage, and then is heard no more;*
> *it is a tale told by an idiot, full of sound and fury, signifying*
> *nothing.*
>
> William Shakespeare

VIGNETTE 35. DECIMELECTION

Brāhmanic Governance

The present Indian electoral system is, in practice, undemocratic: only about 10% of the actual total population back any Act of Parliament. The pretence that an elected Government has *ipso facto* the support of the *majority* is far from valid. In fact, it has only the passive support of barely 10%. The result is that the peoples of India are, indeed, as much alienated from the actual process of Governance as they would have been under Monarchy. Hence, disorder is their only reaction to that which irks them. The much propaganded opportunity to *"throw out the old and bring in the new"* Government leads nowhere because one exchanges virtually identical twins.

Party politics have made a travesty of Elections, Parliamentary Processes, Government and, consequently, Law and Order. The result is pseudo-democracy. The role of money in politics is the determinant in a Society such as ours wherein there is immense disparity of incomes, often accompanied by an even greater disparity of mental capacity and discrimination, *viveka.* Vested interests, dominate the political field. Further, the independence of every constituency's representative is nullified. Consequently, the most morally qualified to exercise their talents on behalf of their country are unable to do so. This is the reason for the disrepute into which Indian politics has fallen. Politics has begotten a lucrative life-long career of, more often than not, ill-educated rolling-stones, instead of being the unremunerated social obligation of every citizen. Besides, there is the only too understandable revulsion that every decent person has, to consort with most politicians and "activists." This alas, is true not only of India.

In the event, there is the tendency towards MAFIA-like organizations with Godfathers abounding and dynasties perpetuating. The *reductio ad absurdum* is the increasingly frequent use made of participation in political processes, from alpha to omega, of subservient creatures only because of the meretricious reason of "popularity" in such fields as Films, Sports and Religious Quackery.

Is there a means to ensure the following: (i) Money plays no role; (ii) Party politics does not foul the nest; (iii) All citizens participate fully, both as voters and as representatives; (iv) There is stability; and (v) The process is simple, economic and open to all? There is. It could be **DECIMELECTION.** It would be apt to define it as Gradual Choice.

What is Decimelection? Political power in a Democracy should spring from and must remain organically connected with the grass roots in Town, Village and Family. There is no place for "ideological" Parties. At present almost all the electorate, and even the common run of members of every Party are unconcerned and even unable to distinguish the tenets of any party. In practice it is Tyranny leading to despotism. Nor is it proper that those who are actually qualified and ought to guide the State are, in practice, shunted into sidings. Naturally, the reliance upon the Bureaucracy is so great that it becomes, willy-nilly, the actual wielder of power without the responsibility for justifying it. Further, it is often frustrated in its legitimate performance and duties by political pressure exerted for the simple reason that the elected Representatives' first and last concern is to remain in the saddles of Power. This necessity has obligated venality. Corruption, at the fountainhead of power, has poisoned the entire politic body including much of the bureaucracy.

The sole means to attain true democracy in India is to treat Families as basic units, including children, because the responsibility for them must be taken into account. Therefore, the basic choice would be from units of 10 votes of neighbours. There would then be 6 steps to select a Deputy for 1,000,000 (10 lakh) persons. At the 5th Step, Deputies for the State Assembly would be elected, each representing one lakh of human beings. At the 6th Step, Members of the Lok Sabha (Parliament), each representing a million, will be elected. They will, thereupon, select 10% of their number for the Rajya Sabha (Upper House). They will, in turn, elect 10% to the Cabinet. The Cabinet will then choose one of themselves, *primus inter pares* (first among equals), as Prime Minister (possibly for a single term). Constituencies would have been automatically determined, census-wise, by actual population corralled topographically, in tens, hundreds, thousands, ten thousands, lakhs and millions. There would be no "Reservation," no pocket boroughs; no pressures; and, above all, no gerrymandering and charisma to seduce the 10 citizens meeting in each conclave.

Political Parties could, if they wished function healthily *outside* Parliament and Assemblies. They would be educative influences operating altruistically through independent media, each of their own. This implies independent Television, Radio and Newspaper networks run by Professionals of all disciplines including Universities, Federations of Commerce, Trade Unions of various kinds and even Religious Communities and service organizations. They are now all virtually gagged. Parliamentarians and Assembly members would vote as their conscience, wisdom and their electorates (of 10 persons) permit. It will not be at the bidding of Führer, Gauleiter, Godfather or local thug. Finally, there will be no monopoly of political representation by coteries, self-styled Political Parties, which are, actually, ideological Tweedledums and Tweedledees. In a highly spiritually developed Society, such as the Indic, the People should prevail. Otherwise, India will be further fragmented.

Each level will have to frame its own agenda and the rules governing their conduct without any pressure from outside. It may also be fairer to women to have a simultaneous and separate say as males at least up to the Provincial level, the assemblies.

Just before, his becoming Prime Minister of India, I spoke to Sri. P.V. Narasimha Rao about Decimelection. I had sent him a Note about it in a purely personal capacity. I had some hopes that he would be interested. I was not disappointed. He called me to talk over the matter. He started our discussion laughingly saying: *"Do you want me to commit political suicide? Do you think that M.Ps will agree to your proposal? It is too idealistic. If I become Prime Minister and you retire from ambassadorship, we can think of a single constituency as an experiment in Andhra."* I didn't want to trouble him further as I would have been no good in Andhra. There is, however, a chance that the present generation of youths can start kibbutzim where, as in Israel, political power does grow from the grass roots direct to Parliaments. Even a single group of kibbutzim can undertake the experiment.

Good ideas, unlike good wines, travel well
the more so when they travel circuitously"
—*Prof Baxi*

INDIA'S FOREIGN POLICY—PERSPECTIVES

Vignette 36. India's Foreign Policy-I

Nehru And His Legacy

THE epoch of blind adulation is happily over. True merits of a great, good and ineffective patriot, born in 1889, can now be Brāhmanically (stereoscopically) viewed. The 25 years before his death in 1964 can be assessed through the consequential 40 years thereafter. For, the Indian attitude begun to be framed in 1939, when, willy-nilly, India was thrust into the vortex of World War II. At the end of 1989, India emerged from the shadow of a banyan under which nothing grew. Its dead trunk continued to be propped up by its two aerial roots. This Essay is hypercritical because crucial analysis is the alpha of scientific study. Encomia are of little moment. They do disservice to the subject: both to the Man and to Time. It is well that, as Nehru would have clearly wished, a compatriot should sincerely record his actions in the traditions of learning that flourished in India till the period we are concerned with. The end of the Nehru Epoch, along with the spectacular collapse, all the World over, of various systems, or at least the most important, gives us pause to cast a backward glance after having climbed to the ridge of this watershed of Time.

Nehru was a creature of his Times. Most historical figures are. He was no aberrant like, say, Xenophon, Alexander, Peter the Hermit, Savonarola, Hitler, or, nearer home, Hyder Ali, Nana Phadnavis, or Hemu. Neither was he a master strategist; nor a clever operator; nor a ruthless, nor Talleyrand as his daughter, Indira almost was. He was a gentleman and despite his use of mythical *Nationalism,* he was a patriot, not nationalist.

Non-alignment and secularism are ingrained Indian Phenomena. They distinguish the Hindu polity. 'Hindu' denotes not a religious but a geographical entity analogous to "Terrestrial" and neither to 'Christian' nor 'Islamic'.

It is this political phenomenon that had led to the abortion or still-births of all native ecclesiae. It is what precludes *a priori* commitment apropos ideas, political, spiritual, metaphysical and applied scientific.

India is, and has been, *par excellence*, the laboratory of the eclectic. Of course, there is and has been the reverse to the obverse of the above medal struck in the mint of Time upon which the legend is: *Sarve Janāh Sukhino Bhavantu; Dharmo Vishwasya Jagathah Pratishta.* (Let all be in comfort; Prescribed Duty is the firm foundation of the Cosmos).

Obviously, the Hindu (Indian) Psyche lacks any positive external or internal cohesion. There is an absence of the 'killer instinct': to K.O. opponents *à* la Tyson or Cassius Clay in the World's Political ring. The unity of India might be capsuled as the power of Negative Rationality: Agreement to Differ. There is also the positive aspect: there is no consequential Parkinsonian eclipse of the socio-political system as has been suffered by every Empire throughout History. India muddles through, survives, re-creates.

Secularism is an much a factor in Foreign Policy as in the internal Management of the heterogeneity that is India. It is its strength. Its pliability is often mistaken for weakness. The logical external consequence of internal *laissez-fair* is **Non-alignment**. In the event, it has appeared, to those who are used to what is termed as *Macht Politik,* power politics. Seeming *ad hoc,* naturally it irritates the impatient jejune: the USA, young, ever in desperate hurry, has little time for the Timeless. France and Germany are, educated by vicissitudes, more comprehending. Ursine USSR, both because of its isolated necessity and saturnine slowness, was more sympathetic, and Russia will anon be empathetic. But for Soviet sympathy, Non-alignment as a world ideology would not have survived. Nehru could perforce not do without the Soviet prop because USA found the weaker Pakistan easier and, more amenable to penetrate. Hence, there was no option but non-alignment for India.

Basic causes for Non-alignment differ from region to region, country to country, epoch to epoch. Only in Indonesia, because of Sukarno and affinity with Indian culture, Non-Alignment was chosen. In Egypt and in Yugoslavia, Non-Alignment was necessitated by equal pressures by the two Super-Powers. When the two blocs' strength changed relatively and USA prevailed, Non-Alignment vanished.

> *No foreign policy—no matter how ingenious—*
> *has any chance of*
> *success if it is born in the minds of a few*
> *and carried in the hearts of none.*
>
> Henry A. Kissinger

Vignette 37. India's Foreign Policy-II

Nehru: Inheritance & Legacy

INDIA is and has always essentially been "an Empire of the Air"—as Jean Paul put it of pre-Bismarckian Germany. He had no inkling of the Luftwaffe! Indeed, 'India' has been for millennia analogous to "Germany" before the Iron Chancellor. India too had a Bismarckian manipulator in Sardar Vallabbhai Patel. There is nothing pejorative in being an "Empire of the Air." On the contrary: an idea is ever the germ of ultimate Reality; India was more of an entity when under a hundred monarchs than it now is as a 'Union'. It has been exchanged for an illusion, fiction for fact. We were one Society, **Indic**, with many governments. Now it is the other way round. Hence, the foreign policy of India, a non-Nation, is nevertheless a unique unit culturally, economically and politically. Its population is too large to be ignored. Hence, it counts as a nation even as United Nations does even though its components are not by no means united.

The prestige and potency of India stood highest immediately after the windfall of Independence in 1947. Why "windfall?" Because of the two World Wars and the indebtedness of UK to USA which wished UK's monopoly of India to cease. UK was no longer able to sustain the expense of re-creating sufficient Military Force to maintain Law and Order abroad. There was no alternative for UK but to compromise by the grant of Independence to safeguard its investments in India, specifically in plantations and industrial units.

That prestige endured for nearly a decade thereafter. Gradually it sank. It plunged to its nadir. The Chinese incursion and India's debacle was the immediate cause. There was a flicker of the guttering candle consequent upon the redemption of Goa in December 1961. There was another upsurge in 1965, thanks to Pakistan's ill fated venture; yet another in 1971, when the bankruptcy of Pakistani statesmanship in Bangladesh brought nemesis to the tyrant, Yahya Khan.

India's relative potency, between 1947 and 1956, derived its power from four factors. First, the non-American affluent World had been devastated and, China had not yet recovered; India was virtually unscathed and initially even enriched by becoming a sanctuary for S.E. Asian and West Asian operators; it was intact from 1945 to 1947 until India's traumatic partition. It was a Caesarian producing twins: West Pakistan and East Bengal, bizarrely attached by the umbilical cord of the Indian heartland! The then already large population of 400 million made India the World's second most populous country after China. That was its second claim for notice. Thirdly: unlike its peer, China, it had not emerged 'out of the barrel of a gun' and abject suffering; nor had it been fraught by a harrowing civil war and internecine dissension. Finally there was Gandhism. Understandably, much is made of what has been called, somewhat grandiloquently, the "Freedom Struggle." The 'Struggle' had not involved even 1% of the Indians and barely 20 metropolises. Of the literate 15% of the total population, barely 5% put themselves out. The 'Struggle' in Ireland was, by contrast, total and ferocious. Nonetheless, the remarkable ideological phenomenon of Gandhism caught the attention of the World's intelligentsia in an Age when ideologies were potent factors. Fascism, Nazism, and Communism had monopolized thinking. They gave place to vulpine Mercantilism. It wears the fleece of Free Trade and has spawned the monstrous Grendels of Multinationals which virulently survive. It was heartening and characteristic of the Indian Psyche to evolve the concepts of *Ahimsa* (non-Violence) and *Satyāgraha* (Appeal to Compassion). They have brought kudos to Indians and provided the spiritual asset to an otherwise almost empty treasury of Political *Savoir Faire*.

The *'Freedom Struggle'* was merely the straw that might have broken the British Camel's back after the poor beast had been battered by two World Wars; when its Treasury not only empty but its assets mortgaged, for years to USA, the heir to her Great Powerfulness. The golden sovereign no longer reigned. Along with, Franc, Mark, Thaler, Rouble, and Dinar, it yielded to the Dollar. Only did the Swiss Franc stand on Its own legs. Worse, British investments in India were in jeopardy, becoming dwindling assets; the role of Middle-man and London as entrepôt collapsed along with its West European market Ironically, as it had partially done after World War-I with the defeat of Imperial Russia and Imperial Turkey. The "Winds of Change," to cite British Prime minister Macmillan's catchy, though by now hackneyed phrase, apropos the Africa of the Sixties,—became a Tsunami. The Red Star rose over China serving Quit Notice to collective Imperialism.USA lost Cuba freed by Fidel

Castro. Some four decades earlier, European hegemony and myth of White Superiority collapsed when Japan called the Tsars' bluff.

Shop-keeping to the last, the Britain astutely salvaged what it could by giving freedom to India. Except for a handful of romantic and rabid imperiomaniacs, it was not regretted. The City of London, ever down to earth, made Virtue of Necessity: investments in India were entrusted to native WOGS, reliable enough, some even played cricket! Britons were assuaged by citations abundantly and deservedly given to the Indian Jawans, Sepoys who had more than proved their mettle in combating the Wehrmacht and Luftwaffe, both Kaiser's and Hitler's, the World's best ever military machine, as well as the Samurai and Kamikaze of Nippon (Japan). That and the ominous ructions within that redoubtable force, the Indian Army and Navy, augured by the Indian National Army under Subhas Chandra Bose. Even more effectively, the brief Naval rebellion of Bombay put paid to illusions of the perpetuation of the Raj. Both the British Army and the British Treasury were reeds broken by Kaiser, Führer and Mikado.

Also to be reckoned was the increasing force of World Opinion. It affected the native British not a little. The Labour opposition, infiltrated by pusillanimous Indian orators, like Krishna Menon and Shelvankar, lost no opportunity to drub the Tory Party whose rating, despite Churchill's magniloquence, was at a low ebb after the Berchtesgaden *cum* Munich surrender to Nazi sabre rattling. Besides, World Opinion was—perhaps still—intrigued if not hypnotized by the Hindu "mystery wrapped in an enigma" that produced 'naked Fakirs' and 'God-men' galore. Educated Indians in the West, immediately before and after Indian independence, were effective. They became objects of wonderment like the Rope Trick, along with the Himālaya, the Elephant and Sanskrit! Cricketing luminaries, mathematical geniuses and Nobel Prizes in Poetry and Science, did more for India in England than mass demonstrations in India. Seldom seen abroad, the Indian woman, demure and debonair, be it Maharani, insouciant ambassadress in Washington, London, less congenially, in Moscow, or winsome wife of Indian diplomat, achieved admiration everywhere. Further, the extent to which, throughout the World, India's hoary Vedic and Vedantic Wisdom including its offshoots, Jainism, Buddhism, and Yoga, her princely palaces, her archetypal architecture, her ethos and her exotica, achieved prestige for India.

Native tinkerers with her Oekonomia in the rat-race to Modernism were regarded as a passing cloud.

> *Foreign policy is really domestic policy with its hat on.*
> *Hubert H. Humphrey*

Vignette 38. India's Foreign Policy-III

Nehru: Inheritance & Legacy

The effect of India after 1947 upon the World's poorer States was palpable: it created a Trade Union of Beggars, the "SOUTH," as against the affluent "NORTH."Some of these mendicant States found therein, forums for their sometimes histrionic, always pathetic 'Nationalism'. Therefore, they clambered on to the bandwagon. Nor was it totally ineffective; the effect was that of a cavalcade, a Tamasha, a masquerade wherein powerlets walked down the avenue of Sovereignty on stilts of self-importance and self pity, stilts often pittances from patronizing erstwhile Great and the actual Super-Powers. The consequence was much ill-concealed amusement, some largesse and barely suppressed contempt. The not-so-very-affluent Patrons were adept enough, and by no means loth to utilize the Non-Aligned Joker in their games of International Snap played at Club Lake Success. Brāhmanically it was a failure.

Few countries had been launched in as propitious circumstances as India in 1947. By contrast, Pakistan was in shambles; Japan, West Germany, Italy and China, had to recover from occupations far more bloodletting than India or any part of India had experienced.

Independent India started off after World War II with the Indian Rupee at remarkable advantage. It was current till the early '50s from Port Said to Hong Kong; this, despite the malicious sabotage of the *asli* Rupiah into the *nakli* Rupiah. It was delinked from silver by the future Prime Minister of Pakistan, Liaquat Ali Khan when he held the portfolio of Finance in the Interim Government of 1946. Thus, though India had a sizeable surplus Sterling Balance, the position of vantage plunged into the appalling Foreign Debt inherited by the Government that took over in the Epoch ending in 1989. Currency—coinage to be precise—is the surest gauge, throughout recorded history, of the strength and prosperity of any state. The *Rupiah*, which had floated majestically in silver sea—13.25 Rupiahs fetching a gold sovereign—gradually sank, a hulk in the Ocean depths of Foreign and native Debt. The Rupee is now, alas, not worth its watermark. The repeated hopes of 7 Five-Year Plans, which provided the rationale for Deficit Financing ended in bitter proof of the Law of Diminishing Returns. Most efforts were sapped by diversions of allocations to profiteers who financially supported ruling Political Parties with a tithe of their takings. Such profiteering was plausibly justified by the continual emasculation of the currency. India's Economic Zone shrank steadily until, even within its own borders, the Rupee reflected it's varying but ever-diminishing value. Thus was the mystique of India eroded. But the undoubted capacity of the individual Indian remained unquestioned. An exodus of Brain and even Brawn, unless deliberately barred, proved that Bankruptcy is what India is heading for: '*Sauvé qui peut!*' (save yourself or sink) was the cry. Undoubtedly there were doughty rearguard actions, several displays of primeval power: the turn in the tide of grain imports; the unbolted djinn of Pokhran; the clean surgical operation of separating the egregious Siamese-twin of Pakistan by giving independent life to Bangladesh; even the Maldive operation of the end of the Nehru age was a glow-worm in darkening days. These are ascribable rather to the soldier, the scientist, the labourer than to Genius of Pilotage. Indeed, how much more could have been done—and can be done—if not a megalithic but a multi-cellular and organic approach were adopted!

The Voice of India In World forums changed from crescendo gradually to echoes in diminuendo. For, meanwhile, the Siege Perilous in UNO was occupied by that very Galahad China, whom Nixon went hat in hand awooing in Peking. Nixon never came awooing to New Delhi. Indeed, Pakistan's cupidity had lit the Sino-US match. The full and ominous significance of a common Sino-Pakistan frontier was brought home, spotlighting the folly of the Kashmir Cease-Fire line perpetrated in 1949, compounded by the virtual surrender in 1972 of the HAJI PIR Pass, recaptured in 1971, leading to the construction of SILK ROAD that joined China and Pakistan and cut USSR off from India. True, there were Indian fingers in the Antarctic pie, in the Law of the Seas, in the Freedoms of the Air, in WHO, ECAFE, IMF, ILO, the World Bank and so forth. Her shallops sailed like wrens aloft eagles. But "the bliss that it was to be alive" in that Age of Hope, the demi-decade of 1947 to 1952, dimmed. Shades of the prison-house closed around India's growing youth. Will-o'-the-wisps appeared to be "Progress." Roots of Gandhism, of Independence, of Indianness were abandoned. The state gnawed into the Promethean entrails of the Indian peoples; Apprentice Zeal waxed fanatic and peremptorily winnowed away all contrary thinking as superstitious chaff.

With the proliferation of World Bodies and their tenancy by more than 160 States, the voices of all but those of the then two Super-Powers, their largest satellites, and of China were inaudible in the Pandemonium of Lake Success. India's was no exception. It too was muted. The Indian presence became routine; her millions no more effectual in the Comity of Nations—to use that high sounding and rather fatuous term—than, say, the Finns or the Turks at best. This signifies. For, the unflattering reality was the gradual depreciation of India: the slide down from the peaks of the Korean Armistice; and of the cardinal conclave at Bandung. Understandably, this decadence has been expensively obscured from the awareness of the Indian peoples by such "Bread and Circuses," such *Tamashas* as Asian Games and "Indian Festivals" that were but passing shows. Foreign Policy was reduced to the absurd. The truth is that unless economic or military power, preferably both, back up fingers in international pies, results are illusory. India did no better, in the event than say Australia or New Zealand with not even 5% of India's 1000 million inhabitants. It is a pity; for, a promising start had indeed been made. The initiative at Bandung in 1954 was the final flicker of a guttering candle. To previously 'Airy Nothing' Nehru, it seemed to some, had given a local habitation and a name. There were notable and memorable Experiments in *Welt Poltik*: a. the concept of Panchasheela[59] (Five Principles), introduced by Nehru at Bandung and welcomed by Chou-en-Lai; b. Non-Alignment; c. the UN ploy apropos Kashmir (albeit a fiasco), d. India's prophetic denunciation of the Partition of Palestine, e. Relations with adjoining States viz., Lankan Imbroglio, Maldives Operation, and f. development of Atomic Energy resources.

---

[59] *Panchasheela (five principles):* 1. *Mutual respect for each other's territorial integrity and sovereignty, 2. Mutual non-aggression,, 3. Mutual non-interference in each other's internal affairs, 4, Equality and mutual benefit, and 5. Peaceful co-existence.*

Vignette 39. India's Foreign Policy-IV

Nehru: Inheritance and Legacy

Succinct analyses of each of the Nehruvian Experiments in *Welt Politik* could be salutary and offer useful guidance to the current epoch that virtually ended in 1989. In 1947, India was riding the crest of world admiration. Even its needless and absurd partition did not affect that overly. The steady diminution of that admiration of India and cessation of adulation of Nehru has, been asserted. With the build-up of Nehru's image, India's actually diminished. It always is the country that suffers when an individual is deified. Nonetheless, Nehru's experiments were remarkable.

The **Non-Aligned Movement** in Bandung takes pride of place. It was opportune. The Bandung Meet was historical. The immediate and vocal support of Indonesia's Soekarno, Egypt's Nasser and Yugoslavia's Tito enabled India to present a feasible alternative to the jostling rocks of Capitalism and Communism. The dove of peace was sent through the Simplegades of *Welt Politik*. But the passage of our *Argo* brought no Golden Fleece back: Then came attempted 'modernisation' of the economy. Significantly, Maoist China's reactions were no more than polite acquiescence. This augured a restricted role for the modified *avatar* of the ancient concept of the Middle Path. Sinic nonchalance was perhaps needed to circumvent embarrassment to Sino-Soviet alliance which did not cool off till Bandung had lost its impetus. Further, had China joined at Bandung fully, would India's role therein not have correspondingly diminished? In the event, it led to *de facto* desertion from the straight, narrow and brambly path of Non-Alignment; it became costly, neither diminishing armament nor retaining U.S.A subsidy. Therefore, first Indonesia and, later, Egypt strayed; Both were netted by US Capitalism. Later, ructions within Yugoslavia surfaced after Tito's death in 1980.It destroyed the cult of both creed and personality. Soon the Non-Aligned Movement (NAM) was infiltrated, plausibly justified by the need for a "broader-base." Actually, it meant that both pro-USA (Pakistan) and pro-USSR (fellow-travelling-Cuba) made of Non-Alignment, an emasculated paper Tiger. INDO PAK conflicts had in fact put paid to NAM after 1971. Such concepts as the neutralization of the Indian Ocean were wrecked upon the atolls of Gan and Diego Garcia[60]. The South Asian Drama became 'stale, flat and unprofitable': India's role dwindled. Then came SAARC[61], a palliative that merely helped to divert attention from the collapse of the axle of the Nehru-Nasser-Tito-Soekarno Quadriga. NAM may now be truly revived only with the concept of Pax Austro-Asiatica, a confederation South Asian States from Iran to Irian counter balancing NATO by South Asia Treaty Organization (SATO) to counter S.E. Asia Treaty Organization (SEATO) conceived by USA with Australia as base and HQ in Manila, former US colony.

Panchasheela was an interesting experiment. Although subsequent events cracked the Sino-Indian urn of *Panchasheela,* which formed the basis of the Sino-Indian Agreement on the Tibet Region of China, the concept itself proved to be an enduring Elegiac Ode, a tribute to the Indian Diplomacy of the phoenix Republic of India. The traumatic *dénouement*, the last straw on the back of Nehru's hopes, was the Chinese invasion of the India in December 1962. The cause of that invasion was, I feel, the reception of the Dalai Lama which was essentially a US exploit. What soured Indo-Sinic relations was the prolonged shelter accorded to the Dalai Lama. His withdrawal from politics is opportune for India. Paradoxically, only SATO can restore Sino-Indic co-operation. It is an ideal goal, worthy of both the ancient Societies, Sinic and Indic (Hindu). Naught in *Panchasheela* can be faulted. It is more pragmatic and specific than the Preamble of the UN charter. The evidence is the failure of every interference of the US Pentagon in the effort to police the world, and be Imperialistic without responsibility.

India in UN: The next Experiment that had important though unhappy consequences was the direct projection of the Kashmir problem by India into the United Nations. It was an ill-conceived miscalculation. Naïveté reached its acme; hopes of justice in US-dominated UNO.

---

[60] **Gan** and **Diego Garcia**: *UK when granting Mauritius independence, agreed to give havens for the US fleet the Chagos Archipelago which were Mauritian. This has encouraged USA to induce Maldives too to oblige likewise, no doubt, for a fee.*

[61] *SAARC: South Asia Association for Regional Cooperation.*

In the event, the Kashmir sore still suppurates. India's brusquely cold-shouldering US embrace (as proposed by Eisenhower), consequently and inevitably, enveloped Pakistan. India had then no option but to lean on the USSR. Had India and Pakistan confederated in SAARC and SATO, the incalculable waste of resources that have since been, and are still, being misspent wouldn't have been. However, India has kept itself almost intact. But Pakistan, apart from its internal squabbles, stemming from anachronistic theocracy, virtually sold itself to the USA. It uses religion as its adherent; which makes the annexation of Kashmir its priority. Pakistan was sucked opportunistically into the maelstrom of Afghanistan. It already had paid dearly therefore. Pan-Islamic Fundamentalism taking root in Pakistan has created disaffection not only among its Minorities, but also allowed decadence in status of women and banned *sufic* spirituality. The pogrom of non-conforming ethnic minorities has emerged from the Pandora's Box of unwise association with Super-Poweredum.

Palestine's Partition: India's stand was bold and clear. Having itself suffered vivisection and repudiated a Theocratic State, India anticipated in West Asia, the aftermath of un-peace and war alternately Hot and Cold. But Indian Foreign Policy was again miscalculated. India lost for decades all the leverage with Israel and, consequently, with the most powerful political lobby within USA. Sops to an Islamic Cerberus was a Chimera, the propitiation of which has actually prolonged internal black-mail and fouled international relations with benefit to none. Both within India and abroad purely secular policy is a *sine qua non*. Internal policy reflects Foreign. Within India there should be no question of minorities after 6 decades of reservation, there should be no continuation of the policy of creating more and more castes. There are only the rich who are becoming richer and the poorer becoming poorer. Calculation of Income is impossible with the currency which is bogus with increase of the printed currency of decreasing value, sheer illusion.

Atomic Energy: The most steadfast course that Indian Foreign Policy plotted and held to has been that on Nuclear Proliferation. Here the palm should actually be handed to the ability, confidence and influence of the excellent Indian Scientists, backed by the whole country including its strategic experts. This was perhaps the most signal and outstanding achievement of both Epochs: Nehru and Post Nehru. The Pokhran Implosion made up massively for dithering fence-sitting, minority pampering ploys which led to cockeyed views of West Asian and

African affairs. India's stance against Terrorism was lukewarm. It earned no palpable Arab gratitude; Indo-Pakistan confrontation continues. It made India look hypocritical to those who had associated India with Gandhism, fearless up-holding of Truth. Within India, so-called Maoists act without restraint. Armed Force can only be answered by Armed Force. The basic truth is that not Democracy but pseudo-Democracy for the profit of unworthy leaders of so called political parties, actually plutocratic oligarchs, prevails. Only Decimelection (see Vignette 35) can oust Hypocrisy.

VIGNETTE 40. INDIA'S FOREIGN POLICY-V

Brāhmanical view

Experiment in *rēal politik* is normal in every State. Foreign and Internal Policies are Siamese twins, impossible to separate. If they are, the rate of fatality is high. It is easiest for despots to wage war; benevolent Tyrants can wage peace easier than Democrats and, quite often, win. We have to admit that in a vast and heterogeneous Society, like the Indic, the will of the people is so varied that consensus is rare. It may be cynically and plausibly stated that democratic government survives because of the apathy of the greater part of the population and their preoccupation with their own individual problems. That which is to be most vigilantly avoided is rivalry within the Party, and, particularly among the most powerful components. No Prime Minister of India can hope to please all his compatriots. Usually, therefore, Foreign Policy becomes *ad hoc.* The Prime Minister has, therefore, to act *sub rosa,* almost furtively. The plus point in India is that it has never been, nor is warlike. There have, of course, been skirmishes between ruling families in the same way as in other continents. Europe was always somewhere or other at war. Total war only came with the disappearance of dynastic Monarchy. Nehru had the advantage of Gandhi's advocacy of *Satyāgraha* and *Ahimsā.* It had the effect of confirming the Old Order within the country until pseudo-Maoism penetrated India. The old *Kshatriya* Monarchy permitted skirmishes between virtual families without disturbing the other pillars of Society. Modernity created Defence Forces. This affected everybody; War has become total. Furthermore, the Forces were drawn from all sections of the people, especially in the higher ranks. It was, therefore, simplest to keep the Defence Forces under Civilian control. This was possible because of a mentality inherited from caste in the Defence Forces. To some extent, contemporary India inherits this mentality even amongst Buddhists, Jains, and Sikhs. This advantage is absent in Pakistan. Another important factor is that the head of the State, the President, who has no direct special interest in the Defence Forces, remains nominal. Defence Forces, mainly the Army, have no truck with *Satyāgraha* or *Ahimsā*.

On the other hand, in USA, the President is in absolute control and is, on the one hand, held responsible for the conduct of Army; on the other hand the President's power is restricted by his tenure and the fact that he is allowed only two of them. In practice, therefore, in the USA, the Pentagon has far greater influence on Foreign Policy because of its being, necessarily, fully responsible for itself and commands control over its prerogatives; it can and does dictate the fulfillment of its desires. Sparring with USSR during the Cold War (1946 to 1975), USA founded its interest to deny USSR its advantages in Afghanistan. The Pentagon was trigger happy; it succeeded in ousting USSR by arming the Taliban. The Civil Government including powerful politicians even in the White House were not happy. A situation was brought about when USA had to interfere as their tools, the Taliban, became despotic. While Russia had been ousted by their surrogates, they became a problem and an Osama confronted Obama. Although the former was eliminated, the continuing return of "body-bags" (US soldiers' bodies) was far from popular. By and large the American people are not bellicose. The pro-war lobby had, as usual, great financial interests. US experience in Iraq, indeed everywhere, from Vietnam to Afghanistan was fundamentally failure. The gains of the Merchants of War were hardly compensation for the ruin of the US Economy as a whole. Likewise, the USA's desire to take advantage of the Sino-USSR rift, and the *rapprochement* between China and USA is serving China's ultimate objective.

These are lessons to be learnt, and decisions to be made thereafter by India's Governments. There have been Indian successes both in the past and contemporarily, for instance in Mauritius and the Maldives. But Gan and Diego Garcia, belonging to Mauritius, matter to India being strategically important in the Defence of the country and its sea routes in the Indian Ocean. Mauritius is and remains, as the French Admiral, La Bourdonnais, over two centuries ago, put it: **"The Star and Key of Indian Ocean."**Furthermore, it has a large and relatively capable majority of the population of Indian origin. Obviously, India has to ensure that its influence is benign and welcome to Mauritians. Likewise, Madagascar and Myanmar (Burma) are closely associated in culture and are also strategically important for Indian Defence. Myanmar's resources in oil, being close to India, would be of immense benefit to both countries.

It is on the economic plane that SAARC will succeed. Instead of concentrating and importing necessities from the West, India can more economically look East and South East. Ancient connections in that direction were of paramount importance to the Indian East India Company of Aihole. Indian ships sailed from all ports in India not only and chiefly to Myanmar but also to Thai, Malaysian, Indonesian, Fijian and New Zealand ports up to the 19th century. They had been welcome and prosperity followed mutual trading. Now, links with Australia will also pay off as Sino-Australian trade has proved. SAARC can counter balance SEATO by SATO.

The conclusion is that we can once again open ourselves to the Pacific Ocean pacifyingly, especially if Sino-Indian relations return to be what they were when both China and India rid themselves of alien gyves.

Vignette 41. Bofors Blues[62]

These may rant and Those may cuss
About the Bofor's blunderbuss.
"What matters it?" the Fuehrer[63] stuttered,
"So long as it has buttered
My party's bread?
Every political herd must needs be fed!
You really should not make a fuss.
Our Democracy is all-in wrestling
Totally unsuitable for any nestling
Who cheeps of Morals peripatetic[64]
In tantrums pathetic! Too pathetic!

So the Boss. The Situation is Gilbertian:
We're being stuffed with empty fustian.
Was the Party the beneficiary
Of shady dealing fiduciary[65]?
Set aside the dull enigma;
We've guessed it all too soon.
Only failure brought the stigma
To our Leader who wrought the rune.

---

[62] **Bofors Blues** *refers to an alleged scandal over the purchase of Bofors guns from Sweden about 20 years ago, legally implicating the very Democratic Monarchic Dynasty of India.*

[63] ***Fuehrer:*** pronounced *Fewrer.* Meaning: *Leader. Adolf Hitler was thus called.*

[64] ***Peripatetic:*** *walking up and down. Referring to Plato, the great moral philosopher, Socrates' pupil, who lectured walking up and down.*

[65] ***Fiduciary:*** *Financial, scam-like*

Dance we to another tune!
Lest on sorrow we should sup;
Hop and skip to the tricky fiddle;
Life's perhaps the only riddle
That we shrink from giving up, from giving up!
Why the exhumation
To rock our Nation?
Congress party will be split!
The Family will be hit
O katrokey!
O katrokey!

Familiar of the Family!
Please do not be extradited
Lest Dead and Living be indicted[66]
And Congress' Fortune be blighted,
The People's wrath ignited.
Be free! Be free!
O Katrokey O Katrokey

April1997 "Acharya of Vidya Kula" (Indian Macchiavelli)

---

[66] **Indicted:** *pronounced Indighted. Meaning:* **accused of.**

GOA'S REDEMPTION

Vignette 42. Goan Episode-I

IFS in India

When posted to Mumbai (then called Bombay) in 1959, I had no idea how welcome the posting should have been. Normally, my colleagues would have considered it "banishment." Home Postings meant goodbye to Perks: Foreign and Entertainment Allowances; and, if you were Head of Mission, a palatial house with extra servants, an official Flag car and chauffeur, gardener, and a security guard. However, in New Delhi there were compensations: picking your next posting by palavers with the topmost concerned; transferring the less satisfactory personnel in your posting, if you were returning to it, and replacing them with choice workers if possible. If you were nearing the end of your career, you could deal with the such matters as getting a site for your retirement or, if you already had a home elsewhere, having a source of good income from renting the New Delhi house out, preferably, to a foreign Diplomat stationed in New Delhi. You could arrange for your children's careers; and, specially, your daughter's marriage. None of these things would you be able to do in Bombay. One usually—I think stupidly—that you will have nothing in common with fellowmen around you, the citizens of Mumbai. Fortunately, not one of the above deterrents mattered to me. I enjoyed every bit of my Mumbai posting.

On Cumballa Hill, next alone in prestige to Malabar Hill, in "Ark Royal" my suite's western windows framed the Arabian Sea. Although Nepean Sea Road ran some 100-feet below, one wasn't bothered by its traffic. My flat was sufficient, its two rooms ample. I didn't need to entertain, as when abroad or even in New Delhi. The sitting-dining room was *à-la-mode Indienne*, **DESI!;** only one long carpet, mattresses beautified by with bed covers and **gol–thakiyaas** (bolsters); low stools sufficed to keep **"thālees"** (dishes). The sole flaws were my huge, ugly bookcase containing some 2000 books and a record player. The bedroom was amply furnished with a mat. I never slept on bedsteads and mattresses, till well after retirement, and breaking my right femur, which compelled me to place a board on a bedstead and spartanly spread a mat on it. The environment was aesthetically ideal; I am an anchorite. My wife and I had agreed that she would live in Bangalore with her father and our three offspring who were his wards; the trio were delighted. There was also an unintended perquisite: visits to Bangalore! officially, every six weeks, to keep in touch with the Karnataka Govt. *apropos* Goa of which the southern half adjoined Karnataka. Karwar was the only entrance and exit permitted by India to and fro Goa. In Mumbai, my household, except when my wife and children came during school holidays, consisted only of my Guardian Angel and Jeeves, Shri P.K. Gopalan, a Keralite from near Panangād, Trishoor. He had joined us and become member of our family in mid-1954. He accompanied us to all further postings. We parted only after I retired and he returned to Panangād. For a quarter century, he had been Māmā (Little Uncle) to our Trio. Without him, we would not have been able, either physically or financially, to make our own home in Mysore: he was as thrifty as we were not.

Vignette 43. Goan Episode-II

Preparation

My job was *sub-rosa*. I was to be a *raw* Nobody. My office and staff were in what was then the new Secretariat in the Southern peninsula of Mumbai on reclaimed land. It was on the first floor, overlooking the garages thereby enabling me to keep an eye on my self-driven car. Once, I saw a man trying to steal something from my car and had him arrested, a service for which I was thanked by the Chief Secretary as many officers had been victims of the thief. My staff was the best I could ever have hoped for. They were all Maharashtrian, completely devoted to their task: retrieving Goa from the Portuguese.

Goa, Daman and Diu were Portuguese enclaves in India from early 15th century. Two more, Dadra and Nagar Haveli near Surat were surrounded by Indian Territory. They had freed themselves a year earlier and made themselves independent. They were not yet officially part of India: no Agreement between India and Portugal had been reached. Unlike Portugal, France had peacefully agreed to hand over their enclaves: Puducherry, Karaikal, Mahé[67] and Chandranagar. They had political, economic, and, most important, cultural interests in India; friendship with India was genuine, both as a fellow Republic and because, like France itself India was eclectic and a source of inspiration to its continent. Olivier Salazar, Dictator of Portugal, becoming despotic, was the obdurate obstacle to any Agreement.

Goa, Daman and Diu being ports, the example of Dadra and Nagar Haveli could not apply to them. While normal economic links were not possible, there was a great deal of illegal "Give and Take" across their borders with India. Particularly, was Goa a god-send to smugglers. Chiefly smuggled from Goa were: gold biscuits, watches, liquor especially

---

[67] Māhé was named after a French Admiral, Count de Māhé, who had had it constructed in the 17th century.

Scotch, automobile parts, and cigarettes. We had about 125 Police **Nāka** (outposts) each with 7 policemen. They became virtually Customs Officers under the Police Department. The Nākas were along the western semicircular border between Goa and India. The arc was from near Vengurla in the north, Castle Rock in the centre and Karwar in the south. Maharashtra was concerned with northern portion, Karnataka with the Southern. Belgaum was the Police Head Quarters.

We had a radio station in **Castle Rock**. It broadcast Indian news and views to Goans in Konkani, English and, sometimes, Portuguese. It was under my charge. We had two personnel, curiously, a young couple: one a pretty Christian girl and the other a patriotic and personable Hindu youth, both unmarried. I was absolutely certain that they were both equally devoted to their work. They led exemplary lives: they had sworn to each other to remain exemplary and marry only after Goa was liberated and became Indian. They kept their word.

We worked closely with the Police headed by Shri. Kanetkar, an Inspector General of Police (IPG). He had an excellent record; he had personally captured many hardened and bold criminals. He was modest and we became fast friends. I too was officially considered an I.G.P. As both Mahārashtra and Karnātaka had their eyes on Goa, I had to be careful not to tread on either's toes. Every Nāka had to be inspected once a month. Its 7 policemen were changed frequently because of the extremely bad environment, their health being endangered by climate and rampant leeches. Besides it was wise for security: their not yielding to temptation by smugglers.

I was given a police jeep personally to inspect all Nākas. This welcome task taught me much about our country of which I had been totally ignorant. Time and again, I found that the further away people were from cities or big towns they were more civilized, trustworthy and honest than the literate and well-off urban dwellers. It is the same conclusion as I had arrived at when cycling some 3000-miles over 3 years in West England and Wales. The hospitality of the poor is genuine, not that of the rich; the poor expected no "rewards."

The area of all Portuguese territories[68] in India was 1619 sq. miles. Their population, in 1961, was estimated at just over 6 lakhs. Europeans

---

[68] **Portugese territories in the East**: *Macao and east Timor between Indonesia and Australia. Vasco-da-Gama, with the help of an Indian pilot picked up in*

were only about 900 in all. Apart from the political effect of Portuguese rule, the interests of the Roman Catholic Church had also to be taken into account. Goa was the base of the Church for all the Dominions of Portugal in the East. It included Macao and East Timor.

Christianity was first introduced into India in Kerala, it is said, by St. Thomas[69], one of the 12 disciples of Jesus Christ. His converts were called Syrian Christians, still an important community throughout Kerala. They were not Roman Catholic. Their Pope was in Antioch in Syria. Only after 2000 A.C, when there was no more a Pope of theirs in Antioch, the Syrian Christians agreed nominally to recognize the Pope in the Vatican in Rome. However, they retain their own rituals and use of Malayālam in their Services and prayers. They also retain their relationship with their kith and kin who remain Hindu.

When the Portuguese established themselves in Goa, they found that there were already many Christians, who called themselves East Indian Christians (EIC). They followed their own rituals and had their own Bible, not accepting the Latin Vulgate of Catholicism. The Catholic Church in Lisbon wanted Roman Catholicism alone to be established within Goa. It sent a priest, Francis Xavier. He started converting the EIC in the Portuguese Indian territories. He was later made a Saint and died in Goa. His relics were kept in a Cathedral in Goa, the only one built in Portuguese baroque style. These relics were considered uniquely holy. Pilgrims came from far and near to worship. After Goa was incorporated into India the relics were taken to Lisbon. Understandably, the Portuguese Catholic Church was apprehensive about the prospect of an Indian take-over. Therefore, it seemed to me that something should be done about it.

---

the African coast, first reached Cochin. Next he captured Goa and Mumbai. Portuguese called it Bombay. It was handed over to the British in the mid-17th century as dowry upon the marriage of their Princess to Charles II.

[69]   **St. Thomas:** *He was one of the 12 disciples of Jesus. He was called "**Doubting Thomas**." He doubted that it was really Jesus who had come back to life after crucifixion and before Ascension. Commemorating him, near Chennai airport, there is a hill called St. Thomas' Mount. Some thought that he was martyred there or somewhere on the shore of the Persian Gulf. It was more likely to be in the latter as Islam disallowed Conversions out of Islam.*

Christianity had existed in India, centuries before the Portuguese themselves became Christian. In Kerala the Syrian Christians maintain that St. Thomas, one of Jesus' disciples, had started conversion in Cochin. They called themselves Syrian because their Pope was in Antioch in Syria. The Portuguese were aghast to find, in Goa large numbers of Christians who called themselves East Indian Christians (EIC).The Roman Catholic Church would not tolerate them. The Inquisition persecuted them; thousands were tortured and killed, if they did not recant and adopt Catholicism. Those who survived fled to neighbouring areas mostly to Mangalore where they prosper. Christians in Goa and Diu and Daman were solely Roman Catholics. Goa became the seat of the Church for all Eastern Portuguese Dominions[70]. It exercised ecclesiastical authority over all of them.

Obviously, it was politic to reassure Catholic converts of Goa and their ecclesiastics. They form nearly $2/5^{th.}$ of the population. Most were poor. They made their living through the males of most villages, working on ships as Lascars. After Britain made Mumbai their chief port, few ships touched Goa. To get jobs on ships, Goan villagers had to come to Mumbai. They were almost penniless. Therefore, hostels were established in Mumbai. They were called **"KUDS"** (called *Clubs* in Mumbai). Every village in Goa had a Kud called by the name of the lascars' village. Those working on ships, mostly as Cleaning and Kitchen crew, were given shelter in their respective Kuds for three days at a stretch at a mere Rupee a day. Kuds were usually on the first and second floors. The ground floor was rented out to fetch money. There was a chapel on the second floor. All in the Kud had to attend the Services in it. No women were allowed entry; neither alcoholic drink nor rowdiness was permissible; the dormitories had to be kept clean by their occupants. The Kuds were looked after by chaplains (chapel priests).

A peculiar feature of the Kuds are teak chests, all kept well away from the walls. Each line consists of 8 padlocked chests. The locks face either the wall or the passage. Two Chests are kept adjoining. Four couples of

---

[70] **Portugese territories in the East**: *Macao and east Timor between Indonesia and Australia. Vasco-da-Gama, with the help of an Indian pilot picked up in the African coast, first reached Cochin. Next he captured Goa and Mumbai. Portuguese called it Bombay. It was handed over to the British in the mid-17th century as dowry upon the marriage of their Princess to Charles II.*

chests were on each line. There were altogether 24 chests. Thus each lascar slept on 4 chests. Each chest being 2ft. wide and 3ft. long and 2ft. deep, there was sufficient bed space. Chests had bushes (legs) below to enable cleaning the floor. Each lascar had a key for his chest. In it, he kept all those of his belongings which he did not wish to take to his ship or, on his return, home. The key was kept in a sealed cover by the chaplain. Usually, 8 chests belonged to same family or friends of each lascar's village.

There was no record of any of my predecessors having visited the Bombay Kuds. It was obvious to me that as Officer in-charge of Goan affairs, I should visit the Kuds and make the Goan lascars feel that they were **Indians** and that they were cared for as such. I visited as many I could, almost one a day. I went to all their bedrooms (we may call them chest-rooms) and even attended Services in the chapels; it made the chaplain and the lascars, who knew that I was not a Christian and was, in fact, a relatively orthodox Hindu, not merely surprised but also happy. The word soon went round that Indian Government Officers were friendly and polite. I had instructed our officers in Karwar likewise to be solicitous and efficient, when Goan lascars passed through the Customs at Karwar.

I found, on the walls of the Kuds, fading photographs of the last King of Portugal who had been deposed before World War I. There was no portrait of Salazar nor any of the Viceroys of Goa. The lascars and their families formed the bulk of Christian Goans. I was sure they would welcome becoming Indian citizens. Only those, who would be unhappy at the disappearance of the Portuguese rule, would be the mafia tycoons. Many of them, actually Indian Citizens, some resident in Goa; they enriched themselves by smuggling, and absence of Income Taxation under the compliant Portuguese administrators, content with their share of the profits of smuggling.

There was also a reliable Goan Catholic priest, Rev. Rodrigues, based in Bandra in the outskirts of Bombay. He was our channel to relay the Indian point of view with regard to Goa, among the lower cadres of the Goan Catholic Church. My visits to the Kuds and the good opinions of their chaplains regarding Indian rule, convinced them that they would not suffer in any way after Indian takeover. All Hindu Goans, except the few rich, were no problem; they would all welcome the removal of travel barriers to and fro India and the disappearance of restriction of entry and exit only at Karwar. The restriction could be called a "negative asset"!

Vignette 44. Goan Episode-III

Brass tacks

It was most important to be in contact with our Defence Ministry. I knew Shri V.K.K. Menon (VKKM) would be most able and helpful to me. He was in New Delhi and in the confidence of our Prime Minister. He visited Mumbai frequently. I had been his host in Oxford. He had been invited several times to Oxford by the Majlis Indian Students' Society of which I had been President from April to June 1941. We trusted each other implicitly.

Apart from formal Reports to External Affairs Ministry (EAM), I was in regular contact with the Ministry of Defence (MD). Shri V.K.Krishna Menon (VKKM) was Defence Minister (17-4-1957 to 31-10-'62).He visited Mumbai at least twice a month. Sometimes, he made unscheduled visits and asked me to meet him at the airport when he was aflight, half-an-hour before he was due to land. I drove my Mercedes, hectically myself. As virtual I.G.P, the moment I left Office the Police kept the roads clear. I would reach the airport within 20 minutes, instead of an hour, to receive him to his great delight. Even in India he was Spartan. He used to listen to me, lying on a board instead of a mattress in the DM's VIP room in Mumbai. He listened carefully to update himself apropos any happenings in regard to Goa after his previous visit. He often fell asleep. One day, waking up, he said "Ah, yes; you are talking about Castle Rock when I fell asleep. Carry on."I became used to this and had my notebook ready to jot down his replies.

The following was the most important happening in the Goan Episode. The Viceroy was Portugal's highest representative in Goa from the time of the Portuguese monarchy. He also controlled Daman, Diu, Dadra and Nagar Haveli. Actually the post was a sinecure: The British had never interfered as Portugal was her "closest ally." However, free India had to keep a tab on all that happened there. Like all countries, including Portugal, we had Intelligence Agents abroad. Most effective agents are nationals of countries wherefrom Intelligence is sought. We knew whom the Portuguese had in India and reciprocated in full measure. When I took charge, one of the agents was a High caste Portuguese Hindu. Let us call him **X.** He visited me at least fortnightly, even when not summoned. He came dressed in pure *Khaddar* (handloom cotton) made famous by Gandhiji who wished all villages to make their own Khaddar and never use foreign cloth which was to be duly burnt at the Flora Fountain in Mumbai, a great *tamasha* for all heart-of-Bombay folk. So, X felt that I was impressed by him as a staunch Gandhian. In Foreign Service, one had to acquire the habit of observing people carefully. I did soon his upper left side *Kurta* was a pocket. His costume was white as white could be, always well starched. There was a hole on the upper right side of the pocket. After a couple of his visits I found that the hole neither changed nor was mended. To him, I was not a VIP. He told me he was always PM's (Nehru's) guest and stayed with him. This blunder of his put me on the *qui vive*..

Once, coming directly from Delhi, he wanted, soon after having entered my room, to go to the washroom and went. My windows were wide open to welcome Gusts of air rushing into the room. X had left his attaché case open wide and the wind blew off papers on the top. I rushed to gather and replace them: blank letter-paper embossed with our Prime Minister's name, National Emblem and New Delhi address! Obviously, taken away for some purpose! I had to act. We had yet another agent in the Viceroy's household. I had gathered from X that he knew "*someone*" in the Viceroy's Office. It was a pointer: **X** could be a **mole!** It was useful to know that he could be double—crossed, and become purveyor of *false* information.

Let's call our other agent, **Y.** Being the cook, he had access to the Viceroy's Dining table. A recorder was put under it. Whenever X met the Viceroy we would know what had been said. I had a hunch that the **someone** in the Viceroy's office would be the Viceroy himself. Hence my precaution; it proved efficacious. I had X followed when he went to Nagpur. He met a VIP of the Congress Party; both were photographed. X was handing over bundles of currency notes of high denomination and the VIP was receiving them nonchalantly. I had met him in Brussels along with an Indian diamond merchant. They were both bound for Antwerp, the "diamond capital" of Belgium.

Money usually flowed for bribery. It was accumulated by Mafia God-fathers who organized smuggling from Goa into India and vice-versa. The most affluent were organizers of the smuggling of Gold

Biscuits. *Gomātā* (Mother cow), was holy. Her Holiness was useful for smuggling. Cows were sent over the India/Goa border before dawn. Grass on the Indian side was inviting. Hungry cows grazed their fill; gold biscuits came out from the ruminants' other end of alimentary canals. The agents, small fry, retrieved the biscuits. It was ingenious. Our *Nākas* did collect some of the "biscuits" for the Government. The tycoons concerned became rich and did not mind sharing a small percentage with their political helpers. However, smuggling was insufficient reason for Military intervention. All we could do was to be content with what our *Nākas* collected. The tycoons were mostly Indians within Goa. They had to keep happy their political friends in India. **X** was the medium. However, it served no purpose to worry about Indians in Goa or India. There was better use for both **X** and **Y**.

Early in 1961, **Y,** not **X,** informed me about a conversation between **X** and the Viceroy. Because of increasing disaffection over Portuguese rule in Goa, both that of the Hindus, tycoons excepted, and the poorer catholic Goans, Lisbon feared a repeat performance of the earlier *Satyāgrahā* agitation of 1955. Our Castle Rock Radio Station and the visits to Kuds had worked!

It was decided in Lisbon that African Troops from Mozambique should be sent to Goa. When they came, they would, being lowly paid, create havoc; especially as they would be no women folk with them, no unmarried Hindu girl would be safe in Goa. This perturbed me immensely. When VKKM came next to Bombay, we discussed our move. He said he would take the matter up with the Prime Minister. What followed proved that he did so.

Soon after, I received instructions to call on the Prime Minister (PM) who was flying to Bombay, and to meet him in Government House on Malabar Hill. The appointment was confirmed. I was duly present. PM had a dinner at about 8 pm. I was scheduled to see him at 7. He remembered our previous conversations including his telling me to join the India Foreign Service, when we had talked in Hindi.

He asked me, as if casually, what news I had for him from Goa. I told him about the prospect of the Mozambique troops in Goa, and the havoc I anticipated. He said that we could do nothing merely in anticipation of "possible misdemeanour." Our conversation continued in Hindi.

PM: *Son, we must have a concrete cause. So far there is none.*

VS: *Supposing something happens to an innocent girl, should we do nothing to try to stop it?*

PM: *What can we do? We can't break International Law.*

VS: *We still have some time before the African Troops come.*

PM: *So what can we do son,?*

VS: *Sir, if it were your daughter or even mine, we would act. We have to*

create a **casus belli**.

PM: *What's that?*

VS: *We should create a provocation.*

PM: *Can we?*

VS: *Yes, I think we can.*

PM: *Do it. Don't tell me. Talk to your best friend.*

VS: *Namasthe ji*

PM: *I'm glad you joined the Foreign Service. I have to go for dinner now. I am already late. Look after yourself.*

He patted me and left..(Original Hindi version Appendix-III.)

VIGNETTE 45. GOAN EPISODE-IV

Finale

I once again received a message from Shri. V.K.K. Menon (VKKM) sent, as usual from his fighter plane, en route to Bombay. As usual I was there to receive him. He agreed with me completely. He told me that, Gen. Choudary of Southern Command, Dr. Baliga a notable Surgeon in Bombay, connected with INDO-USSR Friendship Association and Smt. Aruna Asaf Ali would convene a meeting to which I would be invited. I had met Gen. Choudary when he visited Shanghai and I had presented him some Chinese artifact, which kept him reminded about me. He was glad to meet me and I suggested to him my plan. It was to make our passenger steamer, S.S. **Sabarmati**, which plied usually from Kandla in Kathiawar to Kozhikod (formerly Calicut, Cochin, in Kerala.) via Bombay. She used to steam past the tiny Island of Anjediva (see Appendix IV) (Kānika) in the south Goan coast. My suggestion was that Sabarmati should go as near the Island as possible. The Portuguese had a battery high up on the cliff of the Island. Indian fishermen used to fish all along the coast keeping out of Goan territorial waters. If we could get the battery to shoot at the ship from the cliff, it would be considered a breach of International Law, empowering retaliation; *Casus Belli* (Reason for War) would have been achieved. Prior to it would be agitation in Goa like that which had led to the breaking off relations with Portugal in 1955.I then mentioned my assessment of our **X**, the mole. He should be told about: (a) Agitation in Goa, as on 18th August 1955, when Satyagrahis were shot and some were killed. (b) Sabarmati's sailing, close to the Island. (c) Producing an impression that, as in Dadra and Nagar Haveli, there could be a takeover by the population of the Island. (d) If it were discovered that there was no effective Portuguese Defence Post on the Island, the Takeover would be encouraged. Contrarily, X would mention to Viceroy saying that if the battery were to fire, the takeover would be discouraged. All agreed and duly decided to follow this plan, of course *mutata mutandis* (changed somewhat if necessary). It would be taken seriously and the exact time for action decided. Our troops would be ready on the border of Goa.

I was transferred from Mumbai to London as Commercial Counselor taking over about 18th August 1961. The Takeover took place on 18th December 1961. I had been shifted from Mumbai, as it was considered improper for me as an IFS Officer to be mixed up with Military Operations. A senior Police Officer, a Kashmiri, Sri. Handoo was put in charge. The operation was under General Candeth, who became for a time, Governor of the State of Goa. It was absorbed neither in Maharashtra nor Karnataka.

I was far away in London. I was happy there and feel that both VKKM and the Prime Minister were responsible. After Liberation, naturally there were problems which were in the purview of Indian Administrative Officers (IAS). Accession to India opened up the proper exploitation of manganese. However, as elsewhere, while Tourism does earn foreign exchange, we pay too high a price for it. In both Puduchery and in Goa it would be wise to retain French and Portuguese languages respectively and exchange Sanskrit with Portugal and France for the study of their languages.

WITH GREAT AND GOOD

Vignette 46. Characters-I

Dr. Sarvepalli Radhakrishnan

As an undergraduate, I had met Dr. Sarvepalli Radhakrishnan, (vide. Vignette 32) when he was Fellow of All Souls of Oxford. He had been a "Week-boy" in his youth. He visited China, first Peking and then Shanghai where I was Indian Consul General. As per protocol, I was in the Aerodrome, first in the line to receive him as he came down the steps. Our Ambassador in Peking, Sri. R.K. Nehru, did not accompany him, but sent his wife along with his *entourage* from Delhi. Mrs. Nehru hastened past him, breaking protocol, to introduce me. She started, "*This is . . . .*" Sri. Radhakrishnan cut her short somewhat sharply with "*I have known him long before I knew you.*" From my knowledge of his gentleness, I deduced that the lady[71] must have been froward in Peking. He is one of my Icons.

---

[71] ***Lady (Mrs. Nehru):*** *Before I left Peking for Shanghai, I had to attend the Chinese National day March Past in the famous Tien-An-Men square (The Gate of Heavenly Peace). The March Past was a two-hour affair. All foreign diplomats, chief members of the Government and hundreds of officials were seated on rising rows, of which there must have been at least 10. The standing crowd on both sides in front of us, would have been more than a hundred thousand. Ambassadors and their wives were on the lowest row with their officers' row behind. An unheard of spectacle made this March Past historical. Mrs. Nehru jumped off her seat on to those Marching Past and helping the carrier of a flag, marching past all of us, shouting: "**Wan Shway**" ("Live Ten Thousand Years") till she passed our hearing and sight. Our Ambassador kept his gaze fixed upon Chairman Mao. I don't think that this was reported back to Head Quarters, New Delhi. Happily, the next day, Chinese papers showed no picture. She certainly had been entertaining. Those were the last days of **Hindi-Chini Bhai Bhai** (Sino-Indic brotherhood).*

My last meeting with Sarvepalli Radhakrishnan was in **Rashtrapati Bhavan**, the Presidential Palace of India, with the magnificent view of the distant *Purana Qila*, the Old Fort. Immediately below, were the North and South Blocks of the Secretariat. The Prime Minister's Office, External Affairs and Defence Ministries were in the South Block; Home and Finance in the North.

Ambassadors like me, had to pay their respects to Presidents before their proceeding abroad. He received me most affectionately as he lay in his bed, sparing an hour or talking of old times including our Oxford meeting. Years later, we met in China. Obviously, he was not at all well. Every 10-minutes of the 60, he had so kindly spared me, he requested me to fetch him a bottle of medicine, kept on a side-table, mentioning the precise number. His memory was remarkable and he mentioned my wife's name and asked about her father. He also asked me to thank her for the excellent supper she had made for him, as he sat on an easy-chair in our residence in Shanghai. He had declined an informal dinner on the grounds of being out of sorts. To my wife he said, *"I am sick of the vegetarian dishes which the Chinese take so much trouble to make for me. Your rasam (pepper water) and dadhiyodanim (curd rice) were like amritum (nectar)."* When I was taking my leave, he sat up and asked me, *"Is there anything I can do for you?."* I replied *"Yes, I like you to permit me to touch your feet and give me your Āsheerwādam (blessing)."* He replied, *"Of course, my dear boy"*. I left with a handkerchief before my eyes.

Vignette 47. Characters-II

Sri. Girja Shankar Bajpai

Although I had the privilege, from December 1951 to August '52, of being the personal Political Secretary of Sri Girja Shankar Bajpai (SG), the first and last Secretary General of India. I cherish that posting more than working under any other official dignitary. Sri. Bajpai was titled as Sir. Girja Shankar having been one of the last persons, among Indian Government Officers, to be knighted in consideration of his impeccable and superb capacities. Despite his almost dwarfish stature, his commanding visage and precise enunciation made anyone who met him feel the intellectual power that emanated from him. He had been British India's representative at UNO as from end of the World War-II. His greatness lay in his not been over not being impressed by himself. Jokingly, he narrated to me the following incident.

Stepping out of the UNO building in New York one afternoon he was walking across the road randomly not caring to use the pedestrian crossing nearby. A burly cop stopped him and told him to return to the pavement and use the proper pedestrian crossing. Sir. Girja: *"Do you know who I am?"* Cop: *"I don't know and I don't want to know."* Sir. Girja: *"I am Bajpai of UNO."* Cop: *"Whatever PIE you may be, if you don't look out, you may become mince pie."* Sir. Girja: *"I apologized and did as ordered. I learnt humility. I don't ever forget it."*

Another joke was at the expense of my former Chief in Brussels, B.F.H.B Tyabji, ICS. As Chargé d'Affaires, he was a complete contrast to Sri. Bajpai. In HQ he was Joint Secretary (JS).Every week, SG used to meet Senior most Officers: Foreign Secretary (FS), Sri. K.P.S Menon, and all Joint Secretaries, and me. I was the only Junior IFS Officer present. My business, at the meeting, was to take down decisions, if any, and do whatever chore I was asked to do by the SG. The weekly meetings were solemn affairs.SG usually started off addressing FS: *"Have you anything to say?"* FS would never utter more than 3 sentences. SG: *"Any comments?* Usually, there were none. SG: *"Hm.. Depending upon circumstances I think you may do what you suggest."* The meetings lasted less than 20 minutes. If there was anything serious, he would say: *"A brief Note please; no more than 10-lines if you please"*. My work was simplified. Finally, SG: *"Has anyone anything worthwhile to say?"* Wisely, nobody had. However, one day, and only that one day, JS Tyabji (**T**) spoke up. He was a 6-footer, fairish, and with broad shoulders.

> **T:** *"I don't know . . . But . . . ."*
>
> **SG:** *"What are you ignorant about? Can I help?"* (Suppressed laughter in the audience)
>
> **T:** *"It is what I feel . . . ."*
>
> **SG:***"Well?"*
>
> **T:** *"It is about new recruits of our IFS Officers. They are all so unimpressive."*
>
> **SG:** *"Well, what do you propose to do about it?"*
>
> **T:** *"They . . . They . . . They are all so short."*
>
> **SG***: "I can't do anything about that."* (standing up) *"You see, Tyabji, I too am unimpressive: I am no Goliath. Our Meeting is over."*

I went, dutifully, to keep the door open. Without a word, all exited; **FS** led, **T** was the last. As he passed me, **T** murmured: *"Siddarth . . . Why didn't you stop me."* I replied: *"Couldn't, too humble."*

One unhappy incident, I can't forget. SG told me to draft a Note (Aide Memoire) apropos taking the Kashmir Incident to the UNO. Our advice was to be **not** to go to UNO, until Kashmir was liberated completely. I did my best. SG edited the Aide Memoir and took it to the Prime Minister whose Office was at the end of our common corridor. After an hour SG returned, fuming, via my room which also led to his. He flung the Note. It hit me as I was getting up. SG: *"That Idiot! You have to re-do the Note at once. Say that we may go to UNO. Doesn't he know, UNO is packed with USA's stooges."*

I much regret the brevity of my tenure with SG. I was posted, with the concurrence of the Foreign Secretary, to Colombo. They urgently needed a Head of Chancery and Political First Secretary who knew Tamil. Innocently, I went to SG and told him that I was sorry that **he** had not told me about my transfer. Had there being any flaw in my work? SG: "*Certainly not, bétā, (*son*). The flaw is in the Secretariat. They have no manners. They told me nothing about it. I think I am not wanted here. I shall also be going away*". He was sent as Governor to Bombay.

Vignette 48. Characters–III & IV

Ho Chi Minh And Julius Nyerere

Brief though my encounters were with Ho Chi Minh and Julius Nyerere, I consider them the noblest of the many Leaders of my time. Neither of them tried to impress others. They were the simplest as well. Such characters are rare among people as a whole and the rarest among those most those who attain the summit in their country.

In History, comparisons are not convincing because the facts about them are not accurate. Many are either deified or diabolized. Marcus Aurelius Antoninus is an exception: because it is from his own Meditations and Diaries that we learn of him. He was the last of the Roman Caesars. As a human being, he was more evolved than the great Julius. Some of his thoughts are spiritually quite Indic. He, more than anyone else of the Occidentals fulfils the objectives of the great discourse between Shree Krishna and Arjuna, the Bhagawad Geeta.

There was a difference between Ho Chi Minh and Julius Nyerere. Both were undoubtedly patriotic and cared for nothing personal; not even their designations. Their country mattered, nothing else. Nyerere's was a more modest achievement than Ho's. He was a small-time School Teacher and it seems that what he would have taught his pupils, he exemplified in himself. When he was voted out of Office after his great achievements he simply retired. What one felt for him was affection. He set an example for ALL.

Ho Chi Minh was also a simple man but he seemed to me to be acting a perfect part: he invoked admiration. One would immediately concede that he was too perfect for any onlooker. He also had the good fortune of being linked with the General Vo Nguyen *Giap* of Dien Bien Phu. As for Ho Chi Minh, he went further than Giap who had defeated the French. Ho faced an even stronger nation, USA, a superpower's Pentagon, ruthless and armed to the teeth. He defeated the foe by persistence and by his own personal example. The immorality of the Pentagon was challenged by him and he defeated it. I saw Ho Chi Minh in Shanghai when he visited China and hoped China would befriend Vietnam. Unlike Nyerere, he was not tested by any loss of power in his country. Ho acted; Nyerere was himself. Ho united the two Vietnams, North and South. Nyerere united Tanganyika and Zanzibar, non-Muslim and Muslim majorities, a great achievement.

Vignette 49. Characters-V

Sarojini Naidu

Āndāl, my wife and I had a pleasant surprise one August morning in Old Delhi, not far from Indraprastha College. Indraprastha is a romantic name for an ancient city which gradually grew into Delhi and later expanded adding New Delhi. We had been invited to the *Nāmakarna,* naming ceremony, of the youngest baby girl of the Rāmadhyānis. Tara, the mother was my wife's first cousin. The husband was a senior ICS officer of the British Indian Government. The surprise was seeing the much beloved 'Nightingale of India,' Sarojini Naidu (1879-1949) there. Her husband was an Āndhrā gentleman, a Naidu. Her own name was bestowed to the week-old baby, and Sarojini Naidu (SN) became her foster mother.

SN was very much of a native Indian pearl. She bubbled over with laughter as an oyster does in water. She was very native indeed, and had no Mikimoto artificiality like the cultured pearl of Japan. SN was a prodigy brought up by her Bengali parents, the Chattopādhyaya's. Her mother was a poetess in Bengali. They had settled down permanently in Hyderabad, present day Āndhrā. Their home was the venue to a host of literary enthusiasts. In consequence, Hyderabad became like Lucknow in India or Paris in France where noble ladies were cynosure's for all the literati. She had been a brilliant and precocious student. Her voice was trained for speech making. Her brother, Harindranath[72], was a notable actor.

Soon after her return from England, after her education she involved herself, heart and soul, in the freedom movement, and became intimate with Gandhiji. She had married but lost her husband early, and had no children. Being sufficiently well off, she could devote herself completely to the Congress Party which was dominated, first by Bal Gangadhar

---

[72] *Harindranath had married a sister of Jawaharlal Nehru.*

Tilak and later by Gandhiji. While she was very much a Gandhian, she said whatever she felt about him boldly criticising him unmercifully. She treated us to an echo of what she had told Gandhiji who she called by the familiar name, **Bapu** (father):

"Bapu, you are a complete Hoax! What is more, you know it. Didn't you like being called the 'Naked Fakir' by Churchill? And being so referred to when you were entering Buckingham Palace. You pretend to be simple but you can't take me in. You go so simply into a third class railway compartment, to be occupied by you alone, your only companion being a she-goat and her luggage of hay. You knew very well how much cheaper a first class suite for two would cost the Congress."

She also told us that Gandhiji laughed, retorting that all life was a farce. It reminded me of Shankara's Bhaja Govindam: *Māyām idam akhilam,* (everything worldly is illusory).

Vignette 50. Character-VI

Chakravarthi Rajagopālāchari

Gandhiji was called *Mahātma* (great soul) by Robindranath Thākur which honour was accepted without demur. Chakravarthi Rajagopālāchari[73] (CR) would have shuddered and politely declined. He was, to me, the finest and most enlightened of our leaders; enlightened by both Tamil and Sanskrit literatures. He was a teacher and journalist at the same time. CR was usually referred to with affectionate reverence all over India as Rajaji. He never flaunted his learning or even his feelings. He came of a lower income, middle class *Vadagalai* (northern) Iyengar clan, exactly like my own. I met him in his extremely simple home in T-Nagar, Madras, (now, as formerly in Tamil, Chennai). I had a purpose in meeting him. He lived in a small two-roomed house; it's front door was open. He was sitting with his back to the wall on a mat meant not only for sitting, but also sleeping upon. The pillow was behind him. There was no need for me to ring the calling bell. He saw me, and using the polite plural although I was then only 22, welcomed me and told me to sit with him on the mat. I was not surprised. His gentleness with which he talked to me did inspire, within moments, my affection for him. After my formal Namaskaram with folded hands, I obeyed. My first request of him was kindly to not address me in the formal plural, but consider me as a child, using the Tamil for **thou** instead of **you**. Clearly, what I requested

---

[73] *CR: b.1878, d. 1972. Career: teacher, Senior Congress luminary; Governor General of India, 1947; Governor of Bengal; founder of Swatantra Party after break with Congress; father-in-law of Devdas Gandhi, youngest son of Gandhiji; Chief Minister of Madras Presidency and of Tamil Nadu after the break-up and creation of Andhra; author of several books including versions of Rāmāyana and Mahābharatha. He was highly critical of Partition of India which he ascribed to the Gandhi's and Nehru's ignorance about India as a whole, and its culture, and not overcoming their egoism.*

was greatly appreciated and he, throughout our conversation, mostly in Tamil, spoke to me as I wished.

My purpose was to have his ideas regarding teaching in an English medium boarding school, the Doon School, Dehradun. Despite attractions of the Doon School; especially its nearness to the Himālayā; proximity to Haridwar, and the beauty of the campus, something troubled me. I had *arrières-pensées* (lurking thoughts) about Indian children, not using as medium of instruction, their often beautiful mother tongues and Sanskrit. The latter, because I felt it was the foundation of what Nehru called, in his book, 'The Unity of India'. Nehru himself had made no mention of Sanskrit probably because of his ignorance of it, as reflected in his preference for Hindustani rather than Hindi. I wished to have CR's opinion.

Our conversation mostly in Tamil follows:

CR: *How old are the children you teach?*

VSC: *Between 10 and 15.*

CR: *What medium would they have used in their earlier schooling?*

VSC: *All of them, without exception, would have been taught in English. At home, most of them would have spoken in a mixture of English and their own language. Few in a class of 20 children, solely in their mother tongue at home.*

CR: *Up to what Standards are you teaching?*

VSC: *As I am the Head of the English Faculty consisting of 6 of us, five of whom are Englishmen, I choose to teach two of the middle classes: 7th and 8th. I left the others to teach 6th, 9th and 10th, but also take one of their classes, drama and poetry, myself. I must mention that the others also take classes in History and Geography. Besides, I have the right as Head, if I am free, to help my colleagues in any class.*

CR: *Good. Let me think. There is no help for it. English has to be the medium although I think it is a pity. I have met many young boys and girls who spoke good English even if they had had the mother tongue as the medium in lower classes. But your children's parents make them too anglicized. What was your own medium?*

VSC: *My grandfather spoke to me only in Tamil, except when teaching me English, giving the meaning in Tamil. But my grandmother told me almost all the stories in Rāmāyana and Mahābharatha, explaining everything in Tamil. But our Tamil was mostly Sanskritized. She understood English, but never spoke it. She learnt Indian languages very quickly; wrote Telugu poetry; taught her friends Iyengar cooking in Marathi, Hindi and Bengali. To some extent, I have inherited her ability to learn the basics of some half-a-dozen languages.*

CR: *You were a very lucky boy. What advice can I give you? If you can find a job in a Indian medium school in a language that you know, where English has to be taught quickly in the last 4 or 5 years of schooling, seize the opportunity. You won't regret it. Improve your Sanskrit. I would like to meet both your grandfather and your grandmother. My greatest loss was my mother and then my wife, whom my mother had chosen for me. She did not live to see the marriage.*

VSC: *You bring tears into my eyes. My grandmother died when I was 7½. My grandfather is in Malaya near Singapore. He and my parents and brother, whom I have never seen, are prisoners of the Japanese in our own house because my father was a Retainer Barrister of the British Straits Settlements.*

CR: *I am sorry to hear that. For the time being, be happy in Dehra Dun. Try to spare time to learn the Bhagawad Geeta well. What did your grandfather teach you about behaviour?*

VSC: *Never to tell lies. To consider everything as divine. Desire nothing because the Infinite and Almighty will give you all you deserve, not a tittle more, not a tittle less; don't pray to get anything. You will automatically get all you need.*

CR: *Child, he has taught you everything you need to know. Teach others as he taught you and you will be the best citizen of India.*

I prostrated before him, full length, *Shastanga Namaskaram,* and took my leave. His *Āshirwadams* (blessings) have been fulfilled.

Vignette 51. Characters-VII

Chief of Protocol, Hong Kong

In mid-1968, from Kinshasa, Congo, where I had been Ambassador, I was transferred to the still Commonwealth metropolis-port of Hong Kong (HK) as Commissioner of India. I had served earlier in Peking and Shanghai in China as Head of Chancery and First Secretary Political in the former, and as Consul General in the latter. Having already been an Ambassador, I was virtually Head of the Consular Corps.

HK had much to offer as a free port. All the big traders from Western Europe and USA, who had operated in Tientsin, Shanghai and Canton had shifted their Head Offices to HK, leaving their mainland bases to their Juniors when China had opted for Communism. These bases and their foreign staff were virtually prisoners; they could not move out of China, and even, within China, only with the permission rarely given by the Chinese Authorities. They were hostages. The Chinese wanted to confiscate the property and other assets in lieu of what the foreigners had exorbitantly gained through their sales of opium and other intoxicants, and their encouragement of hostilities in China. These were apart from the Japanese had, more recently, done to China. They also resented the Gun-boat Bible incursions.

One factor which made HK important, was that information about Taiwan was readily available there. Taiwan was not (and is still not), taken over by the mainland and is virtually a protectorate of the USA. Also, it was where US troops fighting in Vietnam were sent for "Rest & Recreation" (R&R). The US Consulate in Hong Kong oversaw other US Island bases in the SE Pacific. The R&R was a nuisance.

The third factor was that our Mission, like all Consulates General, had more than its full share of Consular tasks, plus full time occupation with economic affairs plus assistance to Indian VIPs: HK was too popular as a stopover and our Consular Staff was often expected to accompany the VIPs. While shopping, they used the official transport and asked our Officer to persuade shopkeepers to give handsome discounts. This last was a most delicate affair and caused complaints from both sellers and buyers. I had to put my foot down and, therefore, courted unpopularity with the shoppers and had to answer our Ministry's innumerable queries.

Such a variety of preoccupations fully justified the Commissioner of India being recognized as a full-scale Ambassador. It was as such that presented my credentials upon my arrival to the virtual Head of State, the Governor. I did so and was charmingly received by him. As customary, upon my return to my official residence, I was accompanied by the Chief of Protocol, as it happened, a Brigadier of the British Army. He sat with me and his car followed. Uniformed motorcyclists on either side assured a swift and safe passage.

The Indian Commissioner's official residence was **Jardine's Lookout (JL).** It was one of the oldest and remained the finest of residences. It overlooked the HK harbour, with a view of Kowloon, the bit of mainland China. Kowloon was thickly populated, as against Victoria Island where the Top Notch lived and where the Head Offices of the most important companies, banks and clubs were located. **JL** had been the residence of the Chief Tycoon of Jardine Matheson & Company. Tycoons were also called Tai Pans (pronounced as *tie pahns*) JL had a patio in front of the drawing and dining rooms.

The Protocol Chief (PC) and I strolled out on to the patio where we had the customary champagne and short-eats. We stood enjoying the magnificent view. He pointed at the city stretching 200 feet below us who were on the patio at the brink of the cliff.

> *PC: How lovely it is! A magnificent view isn't it?*
>
> *VS: Indeed it is beautiful. What contrasts! The dark blue of the sea; the light blue of the sky, Oxford and Cambridge colours; and, beyond, faraway all the hills of China with clouds veiling and unveiling the beauties of the mainland".*
>
> *PC: "What about the city below us? We can see all of it at a glance."*
>
> *VS: " Hmm.. Yes. A bit primitive, isn't it?"*
>
> *PC: "Pri-mi-tive?"*
>
> *VS: "Ages ago, men made homes in the caves of hills. Now men make hills round caves and live in them. They behave even more barbarously when rushing in lifts up and down, barely nodding at their neighbours whom they hardly know. And in the mornings there are still floating corpses to be collected on*

those blue waves. It reminds me of Jewish cemeteries wherein granite rocks are stuck, higgledy-piggledy, in memory of the dear departed."

PC: *"I apologise. I confess that I misunderstood your using the word "primitive". I agree with you. I don't like skyscrapers either."*

VS: *"It is the shape of the things to come, dear Brigadier. We must avoid the next War and future Nagasaki's and Hiroshima's."*

The Brigadier and we became closer and closer friends as time went on and both deeply regretted our final parting. I had achieved a coup. As Chief of Protocol, he snipped much red tape in our problems and enabled lightning success in solving them. I am sure he too will not have forgotten our camaraderie.

Vignette 52. Characters-VIII

Dr. C.T. Onions, Lexicographer

I, frequently, but not always, studied in my college (Magdalen) Library after games from 4:30 p.m. to 7 during my Undergrad days, 1938 to '41. Early in '39 one afternoon, at about 5 o'clock, a Fellow of the college, whom I recognized as the famous Dr. C.T. Onions (O) working on the Oxford English Dictionary stood up. He stretched his arms and breathed out loudly. He looked down at me, studying on the other side and quietly whispered:

O: *"Ah.. Our Indian student! I am sorry to trouble you, but can you possibly help me?*

VS: *"If I possibly can, of course, Sir"*

O: *"Let's try. I am looking for the origin of Indian words which have come into English. I am not satisfied with the too little that I know. Perhaps you may know something about them. What is* **Coir** *and how exactly do you pronounce it? Is it an Indian word ?".*

VS: *"Yes Sir, I do know. It means* **'Rope'**. *It comes from Tamil. In Tamil, for most short words, we add at the end, a sound like 'e' in French. In French I would spell the Tamil as* **'quaïre'.** *The last 'e', as in French, is extremely short. Coir was bought by ships' Captains calling at ports in South of India, both East and West. Coir is made of coconut fibre. Is that enough?"*

O: *"Excellent! Is coir the same language in origin?"*

VS: *"No Sir, it is Malayālam language of Cochin and Travancore in the West. Both of them are princely States. Malayālam is derived mostly from Tamil but it is more than a dialect in the west coast. Coir in Tamil is pronounced almost but not exactly the same."*

O: *"Are the scripts different?"*

VS: *"Yes, but both alphabets are derived from the Sanskrit Devanāgari. The immediate source is Granthi. Granthā is a big book".*

O: *"What do you think of the English alphabet?"*

VS: *"It is an awful corruption of the Latin alphabet and much worse than it.*

O: *"Quite right, How did you manage to master English?"*

VS: *" By listening to it spoken by my grandfather.*

O: *"Can you think of any other English words derived from Indian languages?"*

VS: *"Lots. For example:* **bungalow, bangle, mango, calico** *and* **peon** *which has been used in* **Spanish"**

O: *"Thank you.. Thank you . . . It's almost time for dinner, we get out gowns and rush. Can we meet tomorrow at the same time?"*

VS: *"Certainly Sir".*

We parted and did meet the next day. Dr. Onions said that he would speak to my tutor, Mr. Lewis, and my Moral Tutor, Rev. Adam Fox. Would I be ready to spare an hour once a week for the rest of the term at the same time has we had done? I agreed. By the end of the sessions, we had collected some 150 words from various Indian languages, including some from Malay. At the end of my studies in Oxford, he spoke to the President of Magdalen and to my Tutor Mr. Lewis and they, in turn, showed how happy they were about my sessions with Dr. Onions.

My interest in words continues to this day, 72 years later. It helps me to help others learning English in Acharya Vidya Kula School, Mysore.

Vignette 53. Characters-IX & X

M.S. Subbalakshmi and Bālasaraswati

I had the good fortune of not merely listening to and gazing at two of the greatest Indian Artistes of 20th century; and even of hosting Subbulakshmi twice. I shall and endeavour to convey my feelings. It will not be easy because it is impossible to give word-pictures of feelings which are beyond expression. This applies to both the Artistes.

M.S. Subbulakshmi (MS): I met her first in Frankfurt-am-main in what was then West Germany. I was India's Consul General. She came along with Kalki Sadasivan her husband. Their stayed a couple of days. A recital was arranged in Frankfurt and Subbulakshmi's voice succeeded in enrapturing the entire German audience and, of course, all the Indians present. Germans normally adhere to their own highly developed aesthetic standards and values. Essentially, Subbulakshmi was a spiritual singer. She was absorbed by the divinity she invoked. As for me, she drew me into the aura which she spread. The German audience was at first tentatively interested. After about an hour they became more concentrated. Gradually they yielded themselves to *Euterpe* the Hellenic muse of music who at her height appeals universally. There were two encores.

My next experience of the presence of Subbalakshmi was in my home. Once again Subbulakshmi and Sadasivan graced my residence. It was within a week of my becoming High Commissioner of India in Singapore. It was the party of my debut. A couple of days earlier, I had just inaugurated the Chettiar Temple of Shiva. No wonder my final adventure in the Indian Foreign Service, my last post, was blessed by the Almighty. MS's concerts, one in my embassy residence, were all exquisite and ecstatic.

The year before I retired, we celebrated my elder son, Mahavira Acharya's wedding, in Bangalore. The function was held in a relatively small temple. The initial ceremonies were over and the most important rituals awaited. Suddenly a hush fell upon the audience. None of us believed our eyes. Even the *mṛdangam*[74] and *vāzhagam* were silenced.

M.S. Subbulakshmi had come! I had merely sent her a printed invitation. I felt ashamed that I had not even written to her. There she was beaming and she folded her hands before the *Agni Homa*[75]. The *Māngalyam* had yet to be tied, the *Sapthapadi*[76] to be paced around *Agni*. Andal, my wife and I greeted her; MS was garlanded and led to her seat. The holiest rites were performed. MS without waiting to be asked gives us the inestimable gift of her divine voice. All were enthralled. I still wonder if it was not merely a dream, a fantasy. Strange are the ways of Divine Infinity.

I met MS again some years later. Sri. Sadasivan was no more. MS too had retired. I am grateful that I had seen her before she too passed away.

Tanjore Balasaraswati (B): I saw her dance only once in New Delhi. What M.S. had done with her voice she did with her *Bharathanātyam*.

She was, when I saw her, of middle age. Her face was not particularly comely, her figure not at all that of a Bolshoi ballerina. I had seen the Bolshoi troupe perform and been delighted. I doubted if **B** could rival the famed Pavlova. She did more to me than any ballerina did or can ever do.

When she danced, even her first steps and movements seemed to raise me. I was sitting in *Sukhāsana* (comfortable sitting pose) on a mat. When she had danced for few minutes I felt I was being drawn towards her closer and closer; merging into the dance. It was a feeling of entering into a palace of Bliss. I completely forgot myself. All I remember is that feeling of exquisite detachment which the Bhagawad Geetā in its 5th *sloka* (couplet) of the 15th *adhyāya* conjures. Only the dancer was there all else had melted away. Finally, even her body was invisible; only the movements lived.

---

[74] *Mṛdangam: drum, Vāzhagam: oboe*

[75] *Agni Homa: sacrificial fire*

[76] *Sapthapadi:seven steps around the **agni** by the bride following her husband with their garments ends tied and bride having touched with her toes a rock symbolizing the endurance of the marriage.*

No ballerina could achieve that; at her best, I, still young, would have drawn her into me. Our ever-young[77] Terpsichore drew me into her: my ego vanished into ALL.

---

[77] **Ever-Young:** *Balasaraswati literally means the Young Goddess of Wisdom, here the Muse of Dance.*

Vignette 54. Characters-XI

Vaidyāratna[78]

In all people's lives, there are landmarks. The most significant are human beings. I had the good fortune of espying one such human lighthouse which has guided me past many a shoal. It discovered to me the true course in Life's voyage so that my craft did not founder on materialistic reefs. It defined to me my patrimony. It revealed the true Brāhmaṇic prototype; it set my pattern. It confirmed the understanding I had begun to have two years earlier when I had met Rajaji.

Vaidyāratna Sri Gorur Srinivasamurthy came into my ken because his second son and I had married sisters. It is good that, in our culture, such aerial roots meaningfully sustain our nuclei of culture. This rarely happens in other Societies. I was accepted in that large Joint Family of which the patriarch was that Vaidyaratna. When I met him first he would have already descended *"into the Vale of Years"* had he been as most others were; but, in his case, I recollect him still in the ascendant, astride his iron steed, a bicycle, going about his quest like a knight in armour on his charger. His armour was the white *dhoti,* worn in Bombay style, and *kurta,* as immaculate. Upright, as in life, he rode his black mount into the lists of a busy and philanthropic life. He lit me up with the radiance of his visage. And most wonderfully so; his complexion was shining ebony. His intellect beamed at me. He penetrated isotopically, sought reactive comprehension. His was a laser look. To me, he appeared to be the likeness of the deity whose name he seemed so aptly to bear. His darkness

---

78 *Vaidyāratna: Title given to Gorur Srinivasamurthy meaning Gem of Healers.* **Captain Sri G. Srinviasa Murthy** *was the founder of the Madras College of Indigenous Medicine in Madras. His statue in Kilpuak laments what politics has made of Man. He had started his carrier as an allopathic doctor and surgeon with the British Indian Army. He was a pillar of the Theosophical Society of Adyār and cycled daily to its campus rendering his Services to it.*

of hue was resplendent with concentrated sagacity: he embodied *"la Pulchritude de la Negritude*[79].*"* He evoked awe, not fear. He came to the point of an argument with no preamble, no circumlocution, spoke little; unlike, alas, garrulous me!

Indeed, he was a Patriarch. That rare quality persisted long after he was physically no more; for his *"influence"* prevailed, still prevails! The family has not disintegrated. It has even approximated, in his memory. Indeed his is one of the last urban Brāhmaṇic Joint Families, a model for the future when economic compulsions appear once again to have to revive that fine institution for the succour of *"Working Couples"* so that tradition is handed down organically, once more, through dutiful and devoted grand-parenthood.

The last years of this **marvellous** man were virtually non-existent: he spent them in a coma. Yet, I felt that there emanated, from that seeming numbness, a dignity which all the golden finery of Tutankhamen could scarcely rival.

I remember vividly one remarkable incident which would seem to support my view that Sri Srinivasamurthy was Titanic, Promethean. By divine conjunction I was privileged, during one transit through Madras (now Chennai), to be in lovely Adyār in his residence. It was forenoon. There was a sudden disturbance coming from the main road that led to Mahābalipuram. The saintly Pontiff of Kanchipuram, Chandrashekarendra Saraswati avargal, was on his pedestrian way, a golden figure striding on wooden clogs leaving his palanquin bearers panting to keep up with him. Of a sudden, he turned, without any preliminary, into *"Sreenivasa,"* the house of the Vaidyaratna where he had lain, comatose for years. The Holy One strode in, stood gazing at the face of the unconscious form. It was tranquil. Some fifty of us of the family, young and old, had foregathered. He then uttered in a low voice some lovely verses. There appeared to be movement on the bed. He took a bead necklace of the small Rudrakshi[80] off his own neck. He had it placed upon the neck of the Vaidyaratna. Like lightning the eyes opened, gazed back in recognition. Their dialogue of eyes took place silently on the plane of Consciousness. We could not reach it. But dialogue, we felt,

---

[79] **Pulchritude**...: *The beauty of blackness.*

[80] **Rudrakshi:** *Elaeocarpus Ganitrus Roxb, plant sacred to Shiva, seeds of which are made into a rosaries or chaplets.*

there surely was. The Saint abruptly stated: *"It is over."* He raised his hand in blessing all, spun round; strode out without backward glance. And soon the end came, not in agony, not amid lamentation but in ecstasy of reaching the Goal, the *Tiruādi*[81].

The great, fine and learned man embodied the highest Brāhmaṇic tradition. Though seldom seen downstairs in the house where the numerous Joint Family was a veritable gaggle, his presence was felt; he was immanent. As a physician, he took his profession as a prayer. I had been a beneficiary when my beloved four year old little daughter, Ramā Devi, was stricken with typhoid, then still a dreaded ailment. She had been *en-route* to Delhi where I was posted. Her mother, Andal, little brother Viru and Ramā happened to have halted in *"Srinivasa"* in Adyār. The kind healer would not have her budge; he took over the case firmly; he tended her with grand-paternal care and affection. I hastened down from Delhi to Chennai to be beside my little darling. Seeing me so concerned, the Patriarch simply said, *" I am glad you came; you can now help me. She will soon be alright".* And then we talked from time to time on every conceivable topic: Politics, Philosophy or, simply, Geography. He was interested in every aspect of life. I began to be his son and he my revered father.

Ramā was indeed better soon. She crept up the stairs one day to his Study, a mysterious ivory tower, a *Garbha Griha,* Holy of Holies, into which none of us would have had the temerity to venture without his bidding. She found a large sheet with miniscule notes all over it kept down by an inkpot for paper-weight. She, like Newton's dog, upset it and completely obliterated the painstaking erudition that must have been jotted down. The learned man entered, saw, came calmly down with the child in his fondling arms and told us to attend to the mopping up. Of annoyance, there was not a trace.

When he was no more with us physically, it made little difference because he had infused so much of his discipline into us that we strove to merit his good opinion. Such persons are ***never no more***. Their works live and burgeon. Recollection of them revivifies.

---

[81] ***Tiruādi:*** *Sacred feet meaning the Almighty.*

Vignette 55. Characters-XII, XIII and XIV

Retainers

In many countries, called developing, home life is changing. Without exception, all countries till about a century ago, had as an important component, domestic servants. Many of them were women. There used to be, in affluent homes; one steward, over-lord of all the others; he was in charge of the front door and led people into the rooms of the master and the mistress; into the study; he was solely in charge of the drinks and in-coming and out-going letters along with the accounts of the postage for the latter. After the owners and family he would be served his meals and refreshments in the kitchen where his seat would be the throne. He had, almost always, a baton with which to threaten the boy servants like the errand boy.

After the steward came, as Prime Minister, the valet, the personal servant who tackled all the physical needs of the master. The Deputy Prime Minister, who was always a lady, looked after her mistress. Likewise she would lord it over all the female servants and even the cook if it happen to be a she. In the most affluent houses it would be a Frenchman. He would pretend not to know any English to those frequenting the kitchen. There would be half a dozen other servants working within the house and a couple in the garden. At the outer gate, was a retired steward or valet and the wife if there was one. Usually, they were critical of their successors particularly if their wives had been the mistresses' female valet. This description is almost mythical nowadays. It may apply at the most to royal families of the present and past and to multimillionaires. Even ambassadors, male or female, have at most six servitors,—at Embassy expense. At most if lucky, he/ she may have up to 2 'helpers' and a chauffeur from his home country mostly for security reasons. Lesser mortals in the Embassy, up to Minister level and Head of Chancery may be allowed, at the Government cost, one from his own country and one local, the latter usually female.

All this palaver is necessary as my wife's and my experience to some extent was the echo of the domestic economy of yore. In the beginning, when I was of the first batch of IFS and Head of Chancery in our newly opened Embassy in Brussels, Belgium we had to engage a *bonne-tout-à-faire* (maid-of-all work); and another to look after our baby girl and, a year later, also her baby brother. It was difficult to make both ends meet. At the end of the month, for nearly half the year, during the last week of every month, we dismissed our maids at 8 p.m. so that we could be alone to have no dinner, but supper by ourselves. My wife used to tell the maids that she would make some Indian food herself. We then sat next to each other with a cup of milk in between on the table and dipped 3 or 4 slices of bread into the milk and, if the cup is empty, in warm water. We felt well fed having had a bit of Indian mango pickle paste as the final course.

The maid got to know about this frugality. Once a week made a huge can full of vegetable soup for the next days. She also saved up some of the short eats that were left over from the diplomatic parties that a Head of Chancery had to give at least once a month in return for those we had attended. Not to be out-done by *bonne-tout-à-faire* the nurse maid, wife of the door keeper of the Swiss Embassy, did all she could do in her turn. The children of the Swiss Ambassador were taken to the nearby park. Our little Ramā Devi was a show-piece and taken with them into the Swiss home. Rama was barely 2 years and extremely 'handlable' and started speaking French like a native. Her parents became famous and no *"lower case"* party—light hearted ones—were complete without them. Clearly, we owed our popularity to our nurse maid.

Gopalan: Similarly, throughout our life our servants contributed generously to our spending 33 years of our lives happily. To one of them, Krishnan Gopalan, we owe the most. He was almost illiterate; he had his letters to his village, written in Malayālam by a Keralite in our Chanceries. We took him on in Colombo in 1953 from a retiring colleague. Gopalan retired from our service in mid-August 1978. He was a *"Thea,"* not what used to be called "High-Caste". He was scrupulously honest almost to a fault: he saw to it that even a couple of table spoon full's left in a whiskey bottle were not taken away by any server hired for the party; even one cigarette used to be grudgingly parted with. He didn't know his own date of birth. As I was Head of Chancery in Colombo,

I issued him a passport. I could think of nothing better than Indian Republic Day: 26th January as the date. Gopalan was about 25 years in 1954 when he was engaged. I chose 1931 as the year of birth. That made him a year younger my wife (b. 4.1.1930). We chose his place of birth as Trishoor, Kerala. Our parting gift was the small plot 40ft X 60ft with about two dozen coconut trees leaving space for a tiny house. We attended his wedding in 1979 upon receiving his printed invitation sent merely to inform us of his abandonment of bachelorhood. To his astonishment, we rolled up in our van in front of the marriage hall. He ran down from the platform in the middle of the ceremony and I had to haul him up again to make him a husband. Often, one or other of our family, including once ourselves, visit him when going to Kerala. Gopalan was no servant and he always was and will be an intrinsic member of our family.

Lakshmi is another retainer. She has been with us ever since my retirement in 1978; now, in 2013, for 35 years. She was a widow with a little baby girl, Vanaja; she is married and now has 2 sons aged nearly 20. Her family lives within our compound. Telugu is their mother tongue but they are proficient in Kannada, the local language. I communicate with them in Tamil. Lakshmi has become something like a younger sister. That is what our "Retainers" are. They eat the same food as is made for us. We feel responsible for everything they need, including pilgrimages.

Yet, our social life is something that doesn't concern them. There lies the essence of our Indic Society. Despite outward changes, the original objectives remain. My wife's and my objectives are to shed our appurtenances, including the body, into being one with the Infinite; our retainers' objectives are to fit themselves to do likewise.

Buddhi Singh was a Government peon attached to me when in the Publication Division of the British Indian Information Department (May 1945 to April 1948). He was illiterate. He relied entirely upon commonsense and the basic Indic values: loyalty, courage and hard work. *Buddhi* means intelligence. "Little Learning" did not spoil him. During the troubled 1946–47 Delhi riots, because of the partition of the India, it was Buddhi Singh to whom we owed our unaffected life. Although, comparatively his service with us was brief, he is one of our Trinity of Retainers.

Paradoxically, we learnt, from all three, the confirmation of the Truth: Ego has to be shed as a worn-out shred, our worldly ***Karma*** (duties) done, the Ideal Objective may, consequently, be attained.

CANINE COMPANIONS

Vignette 56. Dogs' Tales-I

Humane Friends

All my life, I've doggedly loved dogs. They dogged me to many Capitals. Till I retired at 58, I had one at a time. Then, till 88, the number bred up to 8. Then, alas!, they've dwindled to 2. Every pup was a scream; every diminution, agony. The consolation was that, if I myself escaped into Eternity, their grief would be inconsolable: it would have robbed their *raison d'être.* In vain would they, wait to hear my returning car. So much more is dogs' canine conscience than man's, or even woman's. Dogs' bear their love "even to the edge of doom." So also is their love for their dog mates. Only we, man and wife, console our survivors, **Chin-Chin** and **Tai-Tai**. In Chinese ***Chin-Chin*** *is Gold-Gold* and ***Tai-Tai,*** Chief Lady, our last pair of Golden-haired Retrievers. They are aged 13 and 12. Now, as I write, in the school, which I founded some dozen kilometres and 15 minutes away from our home, I am told they prick-up their ears, from a couple of minutes away, the sound of their beloveds' return, my wife too being with me. Chin-Chin's full name is Chin-Chin-San. *San*, in Chinese, is 3. In Japanese it means Mr. The Chinese 3 is justified by his being the 3rd Chin-Chin.

I have tried to emulate my pets in the hope that some of their doggishness would rub off on to me: sincerity, self-service, vigilance, affection and empathy both in elation and depression. I have learnt a lot from everyone of some two score dogs: to be sincere, never do what their companions don't like. They have an unerring instinct for the unexpected. Instinctively they tell me which visitor can be trusted and which not. I learnt to trust their judgement as much as I do my spouse's, who has guided me away from pitfalls and held my hand in crises.

Dogs know with whom they can take liberties and with whom not. Chin-Chin jumps on to my wife's bed and curls up leaving just enough room for her. As she does not move about in bed she is a good companion. Besides, they are comfortable on mattresses and with quilts over them. Tai-Tai prefers my room. She does not bother to jump up on to the mat on my board. She winds herself on the floor on a mat of her own regularly poking her nose into my mosquito net to reassure herself that I am happily asleep. When I wake up she gives a single bark calling Chin-Chin to accompany her when I open the front door to let them out at 4.30 a.m. They inspect the compound, chase away cats and inform stray dogs outside that they should go to the other side of the road. Having successfully completed their duties, they return for their reward: a biscuit and half a coffee cup of milk, preferably warmed, and the rubbed-down by me with a brush.

Vignette 57. Dogs' Tales-II

Kenneth

My first canine companion, I was aware of, was when I was released from the cradle and finding my feet. Two decades later, I discovered that he had taught me a lesson. I returned to India at 21, hoping to be with my parents in Malaya possibly for my only sibling brother on his 7th birthday, 15th December. Fate, the Japanese this time, had *blitz krieged* (captured like lightning) all S.E. Asia. My nearest kin were courteously made house-prisoners, father having been a Barrister 'retained' by the British Straits Settlements in Singapore and all British territory South of Isthmus of Kra belonging to Thailand.

British Lions and Unicorns proved to be Paper Tigers. Singapore, attacked unexpectedly by land, fell. The British fleet was destroyed by the *kāmikāzéing* of HMS Prince of Wales and HMS Repulse, the most doughty warships of Wave Ruler. I sought a job as Teacher. By sheer chance I was sheltering with the family of my Teacher in Malaya (1930-'34). His eldest son, Harihar, was my "Best Friend" from January 1930 onwards.He continued so to be until he suddenly passed away in 1969. Being virtually stranded, I tried to discover my maternal grandparents. My letter to my maternal grandfather reached him only a fortnight after I had written because he had retired from the Mysore Sandal Oil factory in Bangalore. His reply reached me at the end of December.

He was told that there had been several hoaxes perpetrated by Indian youths returning from abroad. He had to be careful not to be "taken for a ride." Grandpaa requested a son-in-law, husband of my aunt Manjulamma, my mother's second younger sister, to take her along with him to Chennai to confirm my identity.

A fine forenoon, a posh chauffeur-driven limousine drew up in front of my temporary home. A lady of impressive dimensions, *café-au-lait* in hue, resplendent, caparisoned in silk sari embroidered with wide golden border and sumptuous pallu, stepped out. Her diamond earrings and nose stud gleamed, bracelets and golden bangles jingled. Her lord and master remained in the rear seat; his grey hair and severe countenance proclaimed his high rank and status.

Her splendour inspired awe but her kindly eyes and almost shy smile made her maternal. She asked me in Tamil whether her nephew, *Dolly*, was at home. I too replied in Tamil.

Dolly was the nickname, pseudonym bestowed by the 16-year old mother upon her baby boy because he was, to her, the twin image of her beloved celluloid playmate and **bed mate** until matrimony compelled its surrender to her younger sister who was not too thankful because she preferred to play with the living baby, first grandchild of the family. That word survived as *dali* with all cousins.

To my aunt, Manjulamma **(M)**, I **(S)** replied:

> **S:** *I am he*
> **M:** *Do you remember anything about the house in which you lived with us.*
> **S:** *Yes, it was big.*
> **M:** *Of course it was big. It had to house 18 of us. Do you remember anything else?*
> **S:** *Yes, yes, er-er: There was a Big Tree*
> **M:** *True. All houses have big trees. Anything else?*
> **S:** *Nothing else.*
> **M:** *Think hard.*
> **S:** *Um.. um.. yes! Yes!* **A DOG!**
> **M:** *How big?*
> **S:** *Bigger than I was.*
> **M**: *What colour ?*
> **S:** *Black or Brown.*
> **M:** *What was his name?*
> **S:** *I really don't know.*
> **M:** *Think; think.*
> **S:** *Oh! My God! I was only 3 years old.*
> **M:** *Think again.*
> **S:** *Hm.. hm.. it was, ... Yes!* **KENNETH.**
> **M:** *My Darling Dolly! My own Dolly.*

I could not speak. Manjula Chitthi, shorter than me, pulled me down to her bosom and sobbed with joy. She hugged me so tight that there was no escape until she recovered.

Kenneth taught me that even a little child can remember anything important when there is extreme provocation and need to do so. Memory survives from infancy to the end of life.

Vignette 58. Dogs' Tales-III

Rearing

Through "**Kenneth,**" I recalled my riding on the shoulders, grasping his neck, a jogging "Uncle." **Kenneth** trotted close behind as though to make sure that I was not kidnapped. His muzzle was within reach of uncles' ankles till I was back at home on *terra firma*.

Every dog has his or her patent character, foible, preference. Their barks are not the same. Some find their way back. Others, who cannot, wisely await the return of their owners. Chin-Chin-2 went away on his solitary stroll in Mysore University grounds. We, I and two other dogs, had gone with him—Despite my whistling he didn't come. I could wait no longer and returned 3-hours later in fading hope. Low and behold! there Chi-Chin was on the very spot where I had parked. He jumped into the car dodging possible reprimands. Biscuits were what he got.

Not all the English are loving dog owners. Bagheera was a cross-breed, a distant echo of, possibly, an Alsatian and a Setter. He had been grossly neglected. It took over 6 months to re-awaken his trust in Man. He stole food to make sure of a meal; gobbled to satiety when given food. He was reassured after regular food, petting and given baths, and better behaved than naughty children within a month. When we took him to Bangalore to our host's home and left him there, he reverted to thieve. Perhaps, he was missing us and not getting enough attention.

It may seem odd that dogs find a place in Brāhmanic vignettes. There is a misconception that orthodox Hindus considered dogs as *pariahs*[82]. This misconception is completely wrong both about dog and *"pariahs."* In fact, many Indians called strays as pariah dogs, simply because they have to eat offal for lack of proper food. Yet every village has its dogs and

---

[82] ***Pariah:*** *A term, now banned, corresponding to Pagan, living outside the fence; the fence being originally around every village to keep off marauder's, both human and animal during the night. Pagus, in Latin means fence.*

the villagers' consider them as their co-inhabitants. They are respected for their vigilance and they belong to everybody collectively. Even in the epic Mahābhārata a dog follows the eldest of the 5 Pandava heroes, Yuddhistira, when all his brothers were left behind. When he reached his goal, Hades, he insisted on his dog entering with him as he had not dropped behind. The dog then manifests himself as Yama the God dispensing Death and Life. That is why one of my dogs was called **Anubis,** the kindest of ancient Egyptian Gods. My ultra-orthodox paternal grandmother used keep her bedroom door open, bidding good night to brown and white Tommy who was her watchman who never put even in one paw within her room. He had no compunction about curling up next to me until his due hour of being grandma's door-keeper. After me and, of course grandpa, Tommy was her chief concern. Any dog, in its place, is divinely placed. That is why I am vegetarian, Brāhmanically.

Vignette 59. Dogs' Tales-IV

Faring well with dogs

From Kenneth to Chin-Chin San and Tai-Tai, it is 90 years. All our Dogs' tails wag in our memory. Many Rest In Peace, in our garden. Strangely, our elders too, despite their Orthodoxy, cherished their Anubises. My paternal grandma would miss her Tommy who guarded her on the mat outside her open bedroom door; he would never enter the room. She partook of nothing till she had given him a morsel. My Aunt Manjulamma, who had "recognized" me only after I managed to remember Kenneth the dog of my infancy, spent some weeks with us when we were Frankfurt where I was Consul General (1952 /'53). She was *en route* back to India after visiting her two younger brothers in USA. She had been disappointed with her life in USA, and told us it was a relief to get away from there and come to us. My wife really gave her a good time. I put our car and chauffer at their disposal. They had a daily outing, including Wine Harvesting and Tasting, seeing castles, visiting museums and gardens. We three went to the opera and music recitals. No wonder Manjula Chitti wept when she left us and Reckoner, our dog. He had become her's too; she spoilt him even more than we did. Her parting words (in Tamil) were: *"I was so happy here. I would like to be reborn in your house as a **Dog!**"* We had made her to a "caninomaniac."

No wonder the jewels of world of literature is brilliantly inset with Our Best Friend: the four Vedas, *Rg., Yajur, Sāma* and *Atharvaṇa* are depicted as four dogs around Dattatreya; Yuddhistira wouldn't be parted from his Dog even after death; *Qatmir* of the hills of Israel slept centuries in the Seven Sleepers' Den; *Anubis*, the dog-faced was the gentlest Egyptian God; celestial *Sirius* dogs Orion hunting through eons in the sky; even Cerberus could be given a sop! How many a mountaineer in Switzerland doesn't mind getting or even pretending being lost to wait for a St. Bernard with his miniature cask of whisky dangling from his collar. No wonder I "whistle when I work", or am in the dark to **Chin-Chin** and **Tai-Tai**.

Gentle Reader, Bow-Wow to you!

VEDANTIC VALUES IN EDUCATION

Vignette 60. Dharmamananam[83]-I

Intellectually, I would like to say **spiritually**, I founded a school, Āchārya Vidya Kula, equally to Educate and to Instruct. I hesitate to say "**spiritually**" because, I am unsure about the precise denotation of that word. I use it in the sense of Instinct. It corresponds more to Polynesian **Māna** than "Soul" in English. To me, spirituality is quintessence of Divinity. It works subtly; it comes forth from individual human beings; it is felt in contemplation, in **Shanti**, calmness. More than a decade passed before I could discover how Education could commence. How could the seed be sown so that the Child could Father his/her Mind? As Wordsworth wished when his "heart leapt up when he beheld a rainbow in the sky."

The fundamental theory of **Brahmanism** is that the Divine element is found in all life, even in that which appears inert. Divinity is potentially there always. Only, it is not allowed to be manifested by Egoism, self-insulation, from awareness of what is called, in ordinary parlance, "God". It was no use trying to Educate children after reaching teenage. Seeds have to be sown because consideration of what is called "real life" begins to occupy the available energy of all youth. If worldly career is to be the only objective of life, it will not possible for the Seed to sprout. To achieve the real objective of life is to be **Ananya**, unique. Happiness has to be the goal leading to Joy and Bliss, not Pleasure which is transient or even momentary. Life without Quest for Bliss is fatuous.

Such pleasures as indulging in lust; watching games for excitement instead of playing them; playing for satisfaction of winning them, or of making money seem delicious, but are deleterious and corrosive. They

---

[83] **Dharmamananam**: Dharma , in this context it is taken to be **Duty**. Mananam is analysis in the mind. Duty is enjoined in life by birth and environment. Human society is consolidated by the proper performance of Duty of all sections of the Oekonomoeia. The constitution of the original Indic Society enabled this to be achieved most economically.

fatally harvest misery, like injecting oneself to obtain brief physical relief from it. Successfully to educate, one should not pontificate and catechise. The teacher should be Upanishadic and Socratic: questioning and answering both by Teacher and Pupil. Lessons should start with a simple question by the Teacher. In the beginning, only one or two children will answer. Whatever the answer, it should be analyzed. Knowledge, Understanding, Comprehension should be attained by children for them to realize the Infinite Absolute. When they will do so, will depend entirely upon the seed sown, sprouting in the undeterminable future, this birth or the following (vide Bhagawad Geeta Canto VI).

This is the objective of Dharmamananam, our attempt to use Reason and Logic to convince themselves as to what is ethical and moral, and what is not. Pontification and Catechism do not do so: They forbid thinking for oneself. Blank statements, such as "There is God . . . .", do not help; they hinder. A positive beginning could be defining Duty."What is the Duty of a leaf?" would be a promising start. Some Child will know and reply: "Photosynthesizing". The next steps will progressively be to ask for the ultimate Origin of everything. **Vedantically** followed up, it will lead to the Infinite One and All. Understandable 'infinities' are Space, Time, Numbering, and above all, IDEA. Āchārya Vidya Kula's experiment has discovered to its dear children, the **Antharyāmin**[84] in their Jeevātma. However, discovery is not enough, it will lead gradually to realization: they are on the brink of Understanding; Comprehension is yet farther off. AVK has mapped the route.

ALL is uncreatable; it is Creation itself (not Creator!). Neither Space nor Time can be created. Everything is in movement; therefore, everything is, has been, **and** will ever be changing. Change has no beginning and no end. It is eternal. Therefore, it is Divine.

The word Divinity is cognate with Giving (in Hindi **dédo**, is to give up; in Latin dedo is surrender).The Sun gives energy, is a giver, a donor. Hence, the words "Deus", **Deva** meaning God in Latin and Sanskrit respectively, are applied identically to the Sun without the energy of which there would be no Earth and no Life on Earth! That was why in

---

[84] **Antharyāmin/Jeevātma**: is the Effect of Infinite Energy; Boson, the primum mobile, the Prime mover;together they are the Jeevātma, the Human Soul.

the oldest continuous civilization, Egyptian, Ramesis adored the Sun as the total God. But we know that the Sun will itself one day dissolve.

Only **ALL,**
"The One remains; the many change and pass,
Heaven's light for ever shines, Earth's shadows fly;
Like a dome of many coloured glass,
Stains the white radiance of Eternity"
(Shelley's Adonais).

Apart from Ethics and Morals, an equally important objective of Education is to examine or speculate as to what the present generation can do about the contemporary deterioration of morals. What can be done about it, if anything? Education helps through awareness of what is actually being done. The cataclysm of Doomsday has been announced several times even in living memory. For our purpose, we shall assume that it is not in a hurry to arrive. Then we have time to prepare for the best and not for the worst. ***Dharmamananam***, therefore, has to induce awareness of what is actually being done before the collapse of the Global Oekonomoeia. The very idea of "Faster, Higher, Stronger" is plainly stupid. "Calmer, Steadier and Happier" would be more rational.

Instead of Theocracy, or any '-ism', primaevality appears to be the answer. Concrete jungles, polluted Air and Water, regressive population increase make "Progress" imaginary. Merely Technological miracles are no panacea. It is a reversion to simpler and more economic ways of living along with technological miracles that will succeed. Such ways are being tried already and are progressive. Such areas are still minute: Kibbutzim in Israel and in the outskirts of many metropolitan cities in USA, Hamish County, and some remarkable villages in our own country as our Kisan (farmer), Baburao Hazare, recently revealed. To have a future, such communities are self dependent even as were our ***Panchgrama*** (groups of five villages and ***Panchayath Raj***).

Our schools must enable alumni to dedicate themselves to rural occupations and concerns. Our ancestors did so until the relatively recent past, the mid-19th century. Progress, as much advertised, now leads to nowhere near "Heaven on Earth." Omar Khayyam, as translated by Fitzgerald, referred to it some 8th centuries ago. That great mathematician of the early 12th century wrote:

"In and out, about, above, below,
T'is all a shadow show
Played in a box,
Whose candle is the Sun
Around which we phantom
Figures come and go".

Alas! He gave no answer. Hurray! ShankarĀchārya of the early 8th century had already given one:

"Māyam idam akhilam budhwa
Brhamapadam pravisha vidhitwa"
(*"Having wisely realized the World as being a mirage Follow that path which leads you to Eternal Bliss"*).

Bhagawad Geeta, in the final (18th) canto, says how:

Sarwadharmān parityjya
Māmamekam sharanam vraja
(*"Leaving all other concerns, Direct your steps solely to Me"*)

In substance, while founding Philosophers agreed on this conclusion, confusion has been deliberately caused by Theocracy; its purpose being both to Reign and Rule. At times, even Emperors had to bow to Divines of the Ecclesia. Canossa comes to our mind. When Ecclesia could not avoid playing second fiddle, they compromised with monarchy, they supported each other. Only Confucianism in China, and in India, not having an Ecclesia, survived. So too, has Indianism/Hinduism. Some exponents were, Sri Ramakrishna Paramahamsa, Swamy Vivekananda, Ramana Mahárshi of Tiruvannámalai, Sri Aurobindo, Sai Babas of Shiradi & Puttaparthi. None of them had Ecclesia to contend with in India.

Given the above background, Dharmamananam is fully empowered to enable pupils to prepare themselves, and their progeny to re-create **Satya Yuga**, the Golden Age.

Vignette 61. Dharmamananam-II

Exemplary Session: Practical Solutions.

Now, in almost the middle of our Academic Analyses of the contemporary needs of the Indic Society, it is appropriate to discover how we can implement our ideas which are governed by the principles of our progenitors. These principles have led to what Gandhi termed the importance of **Ahimsā**, non-violence, and **Sathyāgrāha,** persuasion by appeal to Truth and Reason. The historical use of such arguments enabled the face-saving exit of foreign rule in India. In our previous sessions, the preceding concepts were logically and scientifically examined and accepted as a viable means of facing contemporary problems which are besetting not only Indians but all the peoples of the World. We have analyzed that the return to **Satya-Yuga**, Golden Age, has to be the basis of both Instruction and, more important, Education.

To summarize: Our *Dharmamanam* has defined **GOD**, not anthropomorphically but as abstract: **Divinity**; not Creator but **Creation** in accordance with the Vedic and Vedantic ideas that have informed our Society. It is the discovery of Intrinsic Divinity of all Life, indeed all Existence, as total Energy. The characteristic of Existence is its Omnipresence, Omnipotence, Omniscience, and its pauseless and unremitting Action causing, therefore, eternal Change and adaptation to ever-changing Circumstance. Progress, therefore, is around a circle or, more conceivably, an orb. Contemporary **Kali-Yuga**, Iron Age, is corroding man technologically: Men are becoming cogs in machines; even Education is superseded by Instruction on conveyor belts called Schools. University Education is longer Universal; it is so exacting and so narrowing and inevitably so. Sophisticated Warfare is economically voracious and self-defeating.

Now, children: we must equip ourselves to face facts and turn the moving wheel of time from nadir to zenith again.

Discussion[85]:

Thatha[86]: *Ananya, what are the ways we can face the future? What are the chief problems we have discussed in our Dharmamananam sessions?*
Ananya: *Increasing Population. We people are using up natural resources too quickly. Our future generations will not have sufficient left and costs will naturally rise.*
Thatha: *Are there any examples of tackling such problem in other countries as well as ours, for example, in America, in Europe or in Asia?*
Sneha: *A good example for other countries will be the **Amish** experiment in Pennsylvania, U.S.A. Next are the **Kibbutzim** in Israel. They lead simple lives and reach the highest degree of culture of the developed world. In India, **Anna Hazare's** village, **Ralegan Siddhi,** in Maharashtra, and **Mathur** in Karnataka all lead simple lives. They live within what they have and need. They don't want anything more.*
Thatha: *Thank you. There are other experiments such as the **Kolkhozes** of Soviet Union? Why were they not successful?*
Kausthub Keshava: *Kolkhozes of USSR (Soviet Union) failed because they were really not "of the people": the Communist Party interfered too much. Kolkhoz members had no incentive. Their leaders were appointed by the party. Many of such leaders were unscrupulous.*
Thatha: *Did any other country try the same methods?*
Koustuba Keshav: *Yes, China did. But while rural areas were progressing, Industries were not.*
Thatha: *Is there any way in which individuals like us can help?*
Kausthub Keshava: *Basically, we should start schools like ours in every rural area, in every remote village and make each one a nucleus centre for Kibbutzim to be formed around them. We should educate not only ourselves but others. They should discuss all matters and everyone will be educated and create their own Kibbutzim.*
Thatha: *Do you think that you can do it?*
Kausthub Keshava: *Yes Thatha. I am absolutely sure.*

---

[85] *(The answers given by the children are only the conclusions on each topic after discussions of 3 to 5 minutes durations. These discussions have not been included)*

[86] ***Thatha:*** *All children of the School, Acharya Vidya Kula, call the author as Thatha (grandfather)*

Thatha: *The Kibbutzim in Israël have been successful and lead a healthy communal life. Our Ancient **Panchagrāma** and **Panchāyats** were guided by Teachers and learned people. Every Monarch used to take advice from learned Pandits. Therefore, it follows that our schools should be not merely instructive, but also educative and advocating an economic way of life as well and freedom of expression. The people of each Kibbutz must be allowed to follow their own faiths and ways of living. But the Kibbutzim should be interdependent economically.*
Are there any highly developed countries where both villages and industries collaborate?

Sneha: *Yes, there are. Switzerland is one of them.*

Thatha: *Is it a good example for us?*

Sneha: *Yes. With a small population they have made a lot of inventions and done wonders. The Swiss live in their villages like Kibbutzim and are well organized like them.*

Thatha: How do they protect themselves? They don't have alliances with any country so they stay away from war.

Kausthub: *They take money from all other countries and keep it safe and people don't want to wage war with them because, if they do so, it is their own money that they lose!*

Thatha: Do you think that this is worth thinking about, as far as our future is concerned?

Sneha: *Yes. Definitely. It is better to try and fail than not to try at all. So we must make an attempt at adopting and adapting this type of government.*

Thatha: *What will you do? How do you think we should constitute ourselves?*

Ananya: *The Union Government must look only into Defence, External Affairs and Communications rather than interfering in every field imaginable. Our country is big enough to have many States which can look after their own affairs.*

Thatha: *Do you think that the UN can play a role in things like Defense, Kausthub?*

Kausthub: *Yes. The UN should be the only organization having an Army and all countries should make their contributions based on their populations.*

Thatha: *Do you agree with him?*

Sneha: *I don't agree completely because realistically it is not possible and every country would want her own pride and prestige to increase.*

Thatha: *Do you have anything to counter her statement, Kausthub?*

Kausthub: *Yes. It is possible if all the countries came to an agreement and form the World Army, to protect, defend and safeguard the walls of this mighty planet.*

Thatha: *Do you think your successors should carry on with such discussions?*

Ananya: *Yes, they should. They should implement this in their daily lives. All humans have faults. We make mistakes every day. So what our future generations should do is to learn from OUR mistakes just as we have been learning from the mistakes that our forefathers have committed.*

Thatha: *My three dear participants. Please, condense your answers and produce, for the next Session of Dharmamananam, a resumé or synopsis. You may consult your class teachers well before our next Session on Dharmamananam Please tell your class-mates that a brief Essay on any topic that interests them amongst what we have discussed, would be welcome. If suitable, it may be reproduced in our Monthly,* **Antaryāmin** *and/or our School Annual,* **Smrthi**.

RĀMAYANAM

Vignette 62. RĀMĀYAṆA-I

Travels of Rāma

The three Sanskrit *Mahākāvya* (supreme poems, Epics), **Rāmāyaṇa, Māhabhāratha,** and **Bhāgavatha** of the Brāhmanical Society (of the Hindus) are isotypical and metaphysical. They sustain the Indic Society fundamentally, from the base of the illiterate through the human literate forests of the slopes and, finally, reach the snowcapped tower of Seers of Infinity, ever-resting in Bliss.

They have done far more than the Greco-Roman Trinity: Homer's **Iliad** and **Odyssey** and Virgil's **Aeneid.** Originally they serve the same purpose: determining the character of their audiences, the *hoi polloi* and the literate elite. For the illiterate, both the Indic and the Hellenic Latin, the six, are mere tales. They connote **naught** else. The Greek epics underwent possibly much changed probably being chanted by the equivalent of bards and troubadours. So too did the *Bauls* of Bengal transmit stories, inevitably adding and subtracting as their memories induced them to invent when they forgot. The troubadours accompanied themselves with lyres. The Indian epics, learnt by heart, diligently by handpicked pupils, were taught precisely by learned *Ṛshis,* seers, in forest-brink and river-bank *ashramas* (hermitages) until they were word perfect; this was absolutely necessary because the Indic epics were meant for more than pastimes are: they were meant to unlock the gates to Wisdom, *Gyāna* and *Buddhi* which led to eternal Bliss, *Sat-chit-ānandam.* Rāmāyaṇa is the most succinct of the Trinity.

The Rāmāyaṇa is ascribed to Valmiki Mahāṛshi,. There is also an even more succinct version, the **Adhyāthma Rāmāyaṇa** which is confined to the final purpose of the original epic, to show the way to the Absolute, the *Parama Purusha.*

Before proceeding to break the code of the ultimate message of the Rāmāyaṇa, analysis of the crafting of the Mahākāvya in *Sanskrit* (culture) is apposite. The perfect epic is *panchaguna,* (has five characteristics): i. *Dhwani* (sound); ii. *Kathā* (story); iii. *Kala* (diction);

221

iv. *Aithihāsthika-ārthika* (historic-economic) and v. *Adhyāthmika* (absolute-spiritual).***Dhwani*** catches the attention of the passersby; curiously they flock to investigate what's happening. ***Kathā*** induces them to listen. ***Kalā,*** the aesthetic rendering of the epic entrances the literati. ***Aithihāsthika-ārthika*** is the historical and economic experience of Indian political science. ***Adhyāthmika,*** it breaks the code by which the seeker of Bliss is given the key to enter eternal repose.

RĀMĀYAṆA-II

Travels of Rāma

The effects of recitals of the **Rāmāyaṇa** are initially hypnotic with its sound and enthralling story. Thereafter, the literati are mesmerized and enjoy the diction, Shakespearean in quality. Then those, who are caught in the net of stocks and shares, and those, who think that worldly Action is civilization, learn of the "Vanity of Human Affairs" and, finally, they are enlightened, having transcended the shadow-show that Omar Khayyam discovered, and are given the key to Bliss. The intriguing mystery of the latter too is worth fathoming.

History and Economics:

As a text book for the above, students of India get a glimpse of Human Affairs. India's economy is essentially agricultural. It had mineral wealth which made its power, both in Trade and in International Affairs, able to cope with economic development and in defending it. The capital of the portion of India with which the epic is concerned is the kingdom of Ayodhya. Its king was Dasharatha. He had 3 wives but no children. Mystic rituals were advised by the holy seer, Vasista. They were duly performed. Four princes were born: Rāma, Bharatha, Lakshmaṇa and Shatrugna. The epic informs us, with the prompting of the astrologers, an interesting future. Normally, apart from the beauty of the diction and metrical beauty, *Chhandas,* one wouldn't imagine anything, remarkable. The story goes on, like a fairy tale, with the introduction of princesses. Marriages take place; but we have not come to the usual end of the story: none of the characters are going to "live, happily ever after". This is when the cryptograph has to be decoded and construed.

Ayodhya, why **Ayodhya?** No war! But how to avoid War? We must be strong, we must have regiments of man and regimen for them. Let's remember that apart from arms, food is also necessary. And then Dasharatha, . . . but why **Dasha-ratha?** As a name, it has never appeared before; it is an invention, surely, with a purpose. Ah, yes! Ten regiments;

let us remember, nowadays, at least 10 regiments are necessary for a city to be unassailable and left in peace. A successor is necessary, an eldest son in perpetuity: a Rāma and brothers for him, just in case. Repeating Rāma again and again—rāmarāmarāma—what do we get in the centre? *āmarā*, immortal! The mystery being de-crypted becomes more intriguing. Patience. You will wait quite a time.

The tale is a long one. Dasaratha goes to War, always accompanied by his most lovely wife Kaikéyi. Amid a scuffle, the axle of the chariot breaks. He will certainly be killed but Kaikéyi rises to the occasion. She thrusts her hand into the hub and the wheel briskly does its job; Dasaratha is saved. He is overcome by gratitude to his beloved and promises her whatever she asks for. She replies that she can't think of anything straightway; but, sometime in future he could fulfill his promise. However, is it possible for the arm of a woman in the chariot to put her arm so far out that it can serve as an axle? Certainly not. It's a clue. It's all about high quality steel, non-corrosive. There has to be monopoly for the purchase of steel in the Principality of Kaikéyā, the Singbhum and Manbhum districts of present day Chhotanāgpur, where iron ore is obtainable abundantly. In the smelting, wood of the neighbouring forest is used. The sap enables molten iron to become non-corrosive. Therefore, the Defence Lobby of Ayodhya determines the budget and virtually is like the Pentagon. The succession too has to be assured as King (Dasaratha) is no longer young. The promise to Kaikéyi is thus explained. The marriage of Dashratha to Kaikéyā is purely allegorical: the marriage is a interminable contract for supply of steel axles, (instead of wooden) between Ayodhya and Kaikéyā. For Kaikéyā, read today's Jamshedpur (the location of Tata's renowned steel plant).

For Defence, not only arms but a regular supply of food is absolutely necessary. Not far from Ayodhya is Mithila. Its people—**Jana**—are mostly devoted to peasantry. Their expert, **Janaka** has invented an economical way of sowing *Godha*, wheat: not merely tilling land and broadcasting the precious seed but sowing it carefully in furrows and covering it up with the upturned soil is an innovation. A furrow is **Sitā** in Samskritam. Mithila's wheat is coveted by many countries far and near. Sita, daughter born to **Jana (ka)** comes of age, that is the wheat is ready to be harvested; several would-be purchasers, including those from Ayodhya and Lanka come to bid for it. The Wheat is of first grade quality; Janaka has used a "golden plough" to make the furrows. Why "golden?" Surely Iron or Steel would be far better? "Golden" must, therefore, be decrypted. It is <u>money</u>, spent for increasing the fertility of the soil with humus, compost and pestifuges. Legend states that Sita was found by Dasharatha when ploughing. He uncovered a female baby, hence, she was named **Sita.** But who really was she? How did she come to be in the furrow? Who put her there? There is a parallel legend in the parallel Rāmāyaṇa. All epics are not by a single author. Valmiki must have been aware of all connected legends and collated them. One explanation was that Sita was actually the daughter of Rāvaṇa, King of Lanka which was a confederation of 10 powerful principalities. A Daughter was born to Rāvaṇa and Mandodari, his lovely queen. The astrologers predicted that she would be the cause of destruction of Lanka and unless the baby was destroyed. Neither Rāvaṇa nor Mandodari could contemplate its destruction. The baby was put into a large basket and kept over the ebbing sea; it was hoped that some fisherman would rescue her. **Vayu,** the wind, told his son **Maruthi** to take her up and deposit her in Mithila ruled by **Janaka.** Maruthi is another name for **Hanumān,** the son of **Anjana Devi,** the Andaman Islands where the monsoon winds whirl. Mithila benefited from the monsoon. We have found that an explanation for not only Sita but also for Rāvaṇa with his absurd 10 heads with only 2 hands with which to wipe his nose. Another legend apropos Sita is also relevant. When Hanumān ravages Lanka before the actual battle of the Rāmāyaṇa, he investigates Rāvaṇa's palace. He enters his bed room where he is lying down beside Mandodari. This lady he finds, rather remarkably like Sita. The only difference is in that the soles of Mandodari don't have the long distinguishing line which Sita has. Truly Hanumān is an observant simian (ape).

The text of the Rāmāyaṇa continues in this manner has to be decoded. It is Rāma of Ayodhya who breaks the bow of Shiva and wins Sita, that is the Wheat, bid for by other countries. Naturally, the disappointed Lankan, being a Superpower, will take revenge. Ayodhyā has to strengthen its Army. The Defence Lobby gets to work. The necessary steel and non-corrosive Iron are vital. The Lobby wishes its representative Bharatha, son of Kaikéyi to succeed. The monarch has most unwillingly to yield. His promissory note (to Kaikéyi) is honoured; Bharatha, son of Kaikéyi, is accorded the provisional leadership of Ayodhyā and the eldest son, Rāma is sent in the direction of Lanka to recruit an Army and strengthen it to match Lanka's. He succeeds. And so the epic goes on.

Adhyāthmika

A different code is used to unravel the hidden message.

Sita here is all humanity, male and female. It is governed by the Senses and the consequent Mind. Decisions which we take are motivated by our inclination and desires which are usually selfishly directed to please the Mind even if the Intellect should be guided by Wisdom rather than Inclination and Desire for transient pleasures; and not for merger into the **Parama Purusha**, Infinite Bliss. Judgment often yields to sinister desires. The only remedy is to concentrate continually on obtaining Bliss, the eternal **Amara**.

Sita, that is We, should control our emotions, sit in Yoga under the *ashoka*(emotionless) tree in the *ashoka vana,* (emotionless forest); contemplating eternity

(*r*)*āmarāmarāmarāmarāma*; Om tat sat, Tat twam asi

ADIEU

The *Darshanaha,*—Vignettes—are glimpses of Divinity that shapes our beginnings. The ends, however, are shaped by our **Karma** (deeds). Our origin is an outing from **ALL**, Infinity. Resulting innings depend on strokes that spin back into the Infinity. Wordsworth in his Immortality Ode wrote about, "whence we came": Heaven, home of eternally happy happenings. Life is fraught by our Senses. They lead or mislead to mirages of green oases and deserts in between in our trek through valleys of rest or tribulation. I keep ALL as my *Dhruwa Nakshatra* (the Pole Star) that the *Saptha Ṛshi,* (Seven Sages) point out. My ship's haven is in sight. It's portal is decked to welcome the Prodigal to be embosomed again by **Purusha** and **Prakruthi,** *Yin* and *Yang,* Divine Nature of ALL.

Here, in this Library, I set down thoughts of the moment, inklings of Visions. Passion is subdued in equipoise, environed by the *"mighty minds of old,"* of those who mused un-bemused of ALL.

I hope all I set down is not mere rigmarole or tedious lecture. My wish is that the Brāhmanic viewpoint be seen: it is eclecticism *ad infinitem* (forever). The Brāhmaṇa, should like, William Blake, *"See Eternity in a grain of sand; hold Eternity in the palm of (his) hand".* He should absorb Wisdom from every *Avatar,* whencesoever it comes. That of the Buddha strove to make Brāhmanism gentle and find kinship in all life. Sacrifice of beast or bird leads to evil *karma,* Sacrifice in War for any reason is also evil *karma.* Even Ashoka's penitence was not enough: like Shakespeare's Claudius, he Kept his all evil gains.

The contemporary, over-Industrialized and under-Industrious Age must teach us not to become cogs in machines or unloving robots, but know how to resume pristine primaevality and be content with the fecundity of Nature, heat of Sun, force of Wind, and *"find tongues in trees, books in the running brooks, sermons in stones and good in everything".* My finale too is:

> *I strove with none, for none was worth my strife.*
> *Nature I loved, and, next to Nature, Art;*
> *I warm'd both hands before the fire of Life;*
> *It sinks, and I am ready to* **depart**
> Walter Savage Landor (1775-1864) 24-07-2013

APPENDICES

I.   Brahmanism
II. Conversation in Hindi with Jawaharlal Nehru *apropos* joining the Indian Foreign Service
III. Conversation in Hindi with Jawaharlal Nehru *apropos* Goa
IV. Anjediva
V.   Aihole
VI. Verses 55-72, Second adhyāya (canto) of the Bhagawad Geeta
VII. Dharmamananam and Kibbutzim

APPENDIX-I

Brāhmanism

Brāhmanism ā la *Vishista Advaita* (Modified Monism). Brāhmanism has different versions: Advaita, Vasishta Advaita and Dvaita. Advaita maintains that ALL is ONE. The modification in Vasihita Advaita is that while it is One, its appearance in the world is of Many like a mirage, and appearances do matter to those who have not been able to perceive 'The ONE (which remains) while the many change and pass.' Dvaita, on the other hand, maintains that the infinitesimals of the Infinite will remain infinitesimals always. As far as I can tell, the phenomenal is so momentary that it is an insubstantial pageant; and Brāhmanic endeavour to perform prescribed duty (DHARMA) with the sole goal of fusion (after fission), with the Infinite. Our deeds, Karma, are but 'Acts' on the World's stage wherein our 'parts' are written by the Cosmic Dramatist, more Aristophanes[87] than Euripides[88], more Moliére than Racine, more Shaw than Shakespeare.

According to Vashishta Advaita, the most accessible path to Moksha (liberation) is 'Surrender' to the Infinite whose Grace (Sri)—the affinity that Infinity has for the Infinitesimal—enables the seeker to reach the Goal, provided, of course, the objective is clearly seen and focused upon and seen: the calls of Dharma (Duty) are heeded and Karma (deeds) are undertaken not to satisfy desire but to fulfill the obligations of birth of the Kula (family stratum) in which previous lives' Karma have sentenced the particular Atma. (The above definition glosses the poem on Vashishta Advaita (vide page xii)

---

[87] **Aristophanes**: *The father of comedy in ancient Greek literature.*
[88] **Euripides**: *Outstanding dramatist of Greek tragedy, like Racine of France*

APPENDIX-II

Why Foreign Service?

नेहरूजी: बीटा कैसे हो? तू तो बच्चे हो.

मैं: जितना हो सकताथा मैं ने किया.

नेहरूजी: अच्छा किया. तो कहाँ पदाई की है.

मैं: ऑक्सफ़ोर्ड में.

नेहरूजी: वाह रे वाह! इसीलिए इसमें कोई अस्चर्या नहीं कि तुम्हारा काम ख़राब नहीं है. तुम ने क्या पदाई की है?

मैं: अंगरजी भाषा और सहियता.

नेहरूजी: वाह रे वाह! इथहिस नहीं?

मैं: कोई भी इथहिस के बिना कुच्छ भी नहीं पद सकता है. आज कल सबसे अच्छा है की इथहिस की जानकारी हो.

नेहरूजी: तू कांग्रेस में शामिल हो जाओ. इसमें कोई शक नहीं की तुम अच्चा काम करोगे न.

मैं: श्रीमाजी! पर शायद मेरे लिए उपयुक्त नहीं होगा.

नेहरूजी: क्यों?

मैं: शायद, मेरा व्यवहार राजनतिझि जैसा नहीं है.

नेरुजी: पर मैं भी तो राजनतिझि हूँ, बीटा.

मैं: नहीं श्रीमाजी. आप तो बहुत सभ्य और शालीन हैं.

नेहरूजी: हा!, हा हा. (*पीठ पर यपयपाते*) तब तो तुम्हे हमारी वदिशा सेवा में भारती होना चाहिए.

मैं: फ़रि भी मैं पहदना चाहता हूँ.

नेहरूजी: यह काम मेरेलिए करो. यह देश के लिए जरोरी है. कुतानीझ बनने की कोशिश करो. केवल तुम ही इस पर अच्छा *thesis* लिखि सकते हो.

मैं: जी मैं परतन करूँगा.

नेहरूजी: बाद में मिलते हैं.

मैं: जी, नमस्ते.

APPENDIX-III

Goa Episode

नेहरूजी: मेरे पास कोई ठोस कारण होना चाहिए I बिना ठोस कारण के कुछ नहीं होगा.

मैं: हमारे देश की मासूम बछियों पर अत्याचार हो सकता है. क्या हम इतने मजबूर हैं की हमें रोक नहीं सकते?

नेहरूजी: मैं क्या करों? मैं अंतर्राष्ट्रीय कानून नहीं तोड़ सकता.

मैं: श्रीमान, इस समय अफ्रिकानी (Mozambique) समूह भारत पहुन्च्नेमे अभी भी कुछ समय बचा है.

नेहरूजी: पर हम क्या करसकते हैं?

मैं: यदि आप की या मेरी पुत्री वहां होती तो हम निश्चय ही ठोस कदम उठाते. हम वहां कुछ स्थितियों का निर्माण कर सकते हैं जिससे उनको यहाँ आने से रोका जा सके. हम युद्ध करने का कारण (casus belli) बना सकते हैं.

नेहरूजी: यह क्या है?

मैं: हम एयसे कुछ उकसाने का निर्माण करना है.

नेहरूजी: हम क्या कर सकते हैं?

मैं: श्रीमान, अवश्य कर सकते.

नेहरीजी: तो कर, मुझे न बता. तेरे सब से बड़े दोस्त से बात कर.

मैं: जी हाँ, धन्यवाद श्रीमानजी.

नेहरूजी: बीटा, मैं बहुत खुश हूँ कि तू विदेश सेवा में आगया. अच्छा अब मैं भोजनके लिए जारहाहूँ. वैसे भी आज मुझे बहुत देर हो गयी है. अपना ख्याल रकना.

APPENDIX-IV

Anjediva

The tiny Island is Kānika in the south Goan coast. In Sanskrit it is Anjadweepa. It is cognate with Āndaman in the extreme south of the Bay of Bengal. (A goddess, Anjana Devi is worshipped in both Islands, east and west of India. She is the Mother of the monkey god, Hānumān. He is also known as Maruthi being the son of Wind god, Maruts, (Aeolus in Greco-Latin); and Ānjaneya being the son of Anjana Devi. As always, such personification is that of Natural phenomena. In this case Maruts, Anjana and Anjaneya refer to the Monsoons, western and eastern. In legend, Anjaneya is said to have borne Sita Devi, (the seed of wheat, Godha) and taken into the Gangetic plain for the people Jana(ka) to cultivate fields for wheat with a **golden** plough; **golden** here signifies the cost of manure and of the work needed. It was seen that Mithila with Janaka as King, pioneered sown wheat in furrows instead of, as previously, being wastefully broadcast. Incidentally, the word **furrow** was taken to denote the ideal length of each line, a **furlong**, an 8th of a Mile.

Appendix V

Aihole

Aihole is a temple complex in the Bāgalkot district of Karnātaka, India. It is a popular tourist spot in north Karnātaka. It is east of Pattadakal, along the Malaprabhā River, Bādami is west of both. Aihoḷe has the potential to be included as a UNESCO Site. It is 510 km from Bangalore and 26 km from Hungund by road. It is one of the most notable places in the history of art of Karnātaka. It is also known as *Ayyavoḷe* and *Aryapura* in inscriptions. It was a prominent city of the Chālukya Dynasty. A place known by the name *Morera Angādigalu* near the Meguti hillocks has a large number of cists (like Egyptian sarcophagi) of a pre-historic period. The place was an Agrahāra (groups of dwelling houses for all of the same Caste). The village had 125 temples divided into 22 groups according to the archaeological Department and has been described as one of India's cradles of temple architecture. Brick structures of pre-Chālukyan times have also been excavated.

It must have been a commercial centre and the headquarters of the Deccan East India Company. Aihole was chosen chiefly because it was a temple city, inhabited solely by Brāhmins and so it was guarded, as it were, by superstition. The Merchants' stocks could be left safely there. Elsewhere, they would have to be guarded, expensively, hoping that the guards themselves would be trustworthy. Later, the British asked for and obtained permission from the Muslim rulers to construct forts such as Fort St. George in Madras (Chennai). Muslim rulers made the mistake of not levying any land tax and thus enabled the Factors to consider it as their own territory

APPENDIX-VI

Verses 55-72, Second adhyāya (canto) of the Bhagawad Geeta

v54: (Arjuna) What, O Keshava, distinguishes the one of steadfast wisdom, steeped in Samadhi? How does one of firm wisdom speak, how sit, how walk?

The **Lord Krishna** answers:

v55: When one abandons, O Partha, all heartfelt desire and is content in the Self by the Self, then is the one recognized as stable in wisdom.

v56: He whose mind is not perturbed by adversity, craves not for pleasure, free from fondness, fear and anger, such is the Seer of absolute Wisdom.

v57: He who is ever free from attachment, who is not affected by receiving good nor dejected by bad, is equip-poised in Wisdom.

v58: When too, like a tortoise its limbs, he withdraws his senses from sense-objects, his wisdom is set firmly.

v59: Sense objects vanish for the abstinent man, though not the longing for them. His longing too ceases when he realizes the Supreme.

v60: Excited senses, O son of Kunti, impetuously decoy the mind of even the wise, while striving for perfection.

v61: The Yogi, having controlled all senses is focussed on ALL alone as the supreme goal. His wisdom is perpetual whose senses are subjugated.

v62: Brooding on cravings of the Senses, man's attachment to them develops; from attachments springs desire; from desire sprouts anger.

v63: From anger proceeds delusion; from delusion, confused memory; from confused memory ruin of Reason; with reason ruined he utterly perishes.

v64: But the disciplined Yogi, even environed by pleasures has senses under control, free from both attraction and aversion, he grows in tranquillity.

v65: In tranquillity, sorrow is destroyed. For the intellect of the tranquil-minded is firmly anchored in equilibrium.

v66: There is no wisdom in the fickle-minded; nor any meditation in him. To the un-meditative there is no peace. How then the peace less enjoy happiness?

v67: Just as a gale pushes a ship away on the billows, the mind yields to the roving senses and carries away his discrimination.

v68: Therefore, O mighty-armed, his cognition is well poised, whose senses are completely unaffected.

v69: That which is night to all beings, in that the disciplined man is awake; that in which all beings wake, is night to the eternal seer.

v70: Not craving fulfilment of desire, man attains Peace. In him all desires merge even as rivers flow into the ocean full and unmoving.

v71: That man attains Peace who lives devoid of longing, freed from all desires and without the feeling of "I" and "mine".

v72: This, O Parthia, is the Brāhmanic state. Attaining Nirvāṇa, none is bewildered. Established in it even at the hour of death, this seer gains oneness with Brahman.

APPENDIX-VII

Dharmamananam and Kibbutzim

There have been many townships created during the last century in India which could develop into Kibbutzim. Thereby, they would help to solve problems encountered in our still fledgling Republic of India. Examples are: the Jamshedpur Tata steel township and Aurobindo Auroville near Puducherry. However, these townships were founded "top-downwards": their grassroots didn't exist. They didn't operate as political units as the Kibbutzim in Israel had done as from 1910. In India, it is the villagers who have to be evolved into a comprehensive whole, thereby doing away with political Parties. Gandhiji was right in stressing the rural base of India.

The Kibbutzim, discussed in Dharamamananam, have their prototype, closest to our conception of the future of India, incorruptible politically, in **Mathur** near Shimoga mentioned by Sneha in the Exemplary Session.

Mathur is a remarkable village within Karnataka itself. It is near Shimoga. A community called **Sanketi** settled some 5 centuries ago in 5 villages at the request of the then Maharaja of part of what is now Karnataka. Of these, known to me is Mathur on the Thunga river's left bank. Opposite, on the right bank, also Sanketi, is Hosahalli. They are renowned for being totally Sanskrit speaking. I am reliably told there are still traces of the other three villages surviving. People from all over the world keep visiting Mathur because of Sanskrit being solely spoken in it. It is equally famous for **Gamaka** school of chanting in Sanskrit.

I was honoured by being invited to visit Mathur about 25 years ago. The remarkable thing is that they are no people in Mathur other than Sanketis. All types of work are done by them who are all Brahmins. This little village has produced several highly skilled people, including several Ph.Ds. Many have gone to America but always return to the village. There were only two cars owned by Medical Doctors working in Shimoga; one is left in Mathur as a First Aid reserve.

I asked whether those who were in America helped the village monetarily. Laughingly, I was told that, apart from personal gifts to relatives, no help was received or needed. In fact, the visitors went back loaded with gifts. Apart from various remittances from within India all families were independent because of their adjoining areca nut plantations cultivated by expert contract labour from Tamil Nadu for 11 months each year. There was only one TV set common to all kept in the hall of the Head of the village. There is 100% literacy. They run their own school.

There had been absolutely no crime at all and no need for a Police Station. In fact, Mathur and, presumably also Hosahalli, were like independent Kibbutzim. The Head of the Bharatiya Vidya Bhawan (BVB) in London, the late Sri. Mathur Krishnamurthy, was from Mathur. After retirement till his passing away in 2012, he was Head of the BVB in Bangalore. He had visited Acharya Vidya Kula. Smt. Shruthi, Music Mistress in AVK, is a Sanketi and an expert in **Gamaka**.

Mathur is an excellent example of what can be done by our youth to revolutionize politics in our country and remove corruption. There is no reason why the Alumni of Acharya Vidya Kula can't rival Mathur.

INDEX